THE ADVENTUROUS BOOK OF OUTDOOR GAMES

Classic Fun for Daring Boys and Girls

SCOTT STROTHER

SOURCEBOOKS, INC.
NAPERVILLE, ILLINOIS

Published by Sourcebooks, Inc.
P.O. Box 4410, Naperville, Illinois 60567-4410
(630) 961-3900
Fax: (630) 961-2168
www.sourcebooks.com

Library of Congress Cataloging-in-Publication Data

Strother, Scott.
   The adventurous book of outdoor games : classic fun for daring boys and girls / Scott
Strother.
       p. cm.
 1. Outdoor games. I. Title.
   GV1203.S775 2008
   796—dc22
                                        2008015077

Printed and bound in the United States of America.
VP 10 9 8 7 6 5 4 3 2 1

To my neighbors in Westerville, Ohio, for playing these games with me for hours every day. To the children in my tennis lessons, for inspiring me to write this book. And to all my friends and family who supported the book, especially my mother, who taught many of the games to everyone in our neighborhood.

CONTENTS

A NOTE FOR PARENTS

Two powerful motivations inspired me to create this book. The first inspiration came during the last few summers that I worked as a tennis coach and instructor. I taught kids aged six to sixteen (those who will get the most use from this book). The children and I would have fun together, especially when I taught them creative tennis games. One day, I began talking to a few of my students about other fun games I used to play around my neighborhood. You would not believe the blank stares of bewilderment that lay upon me as I mentioned Ghost in the Graveyard and even Kick the Can. This was too much for me to handle. Why? I will come to that shortly.

The second inspiration came while I was writing a paper on childhood obesity. In the back of my mind, I had always noticed what seemed to be an increase in this problem. As I researched the topic, I was amazed at how bad the problem really has become. I will not bore you with the lengthy facts and details, but childhood obesity is reaching epidemic proportions. This is partially because of the increase in fast food and video games that cause a lack of exercise, poor food choices, and overall decreased health. The adverse effects of childhood obesity are too strong to be ignored.

The combination of this dilemma and children's unawareness of these outdoor games felt like a smack in the face. The games in this book are simply too much fun and offer too many positive rewards to be set aside for video games. It bothers me to think that kids are not outside enjoying them.

Let me briefly describe my childhood to help explain my enthusiasm for the games included in this book. I grew up in a neighborhood that I loved tremendously. This is mostly because of the activities in which I found myself involved. Every night after dinner, and often during the day, kids from all over the neighborhood would come out and gather near my house. If people did not meet, we would go out and find anyone and everyone. Each time, we would all organize a large game for everyone to play. I will not discuss which games (because they are all described in this book!), but I loved them all. It was not just the games, but getting together with friends, making new friends, exercising, being outside, *and* doing a fun activity that made the process so enjoyable. Other kids felt the exact same way, which is why no one could stay away.

The more I thought about how much fun I used to have, the more amazed I was that many kids today are not enjoying these activities. When I look back upon growing up, these games are a large part of my memories. Once children get into a routine of playing the games in this book, it should elate them as it did me. Even if children already know some of the games, this book offers an enormous variety of new, exciting ones that they can learn and play.

Learning and playing these games will be great for kids in more ways than you can imagine. It might take a little effort at first, learning the games and getting other children to play, but once kids start learning these exciting games, they will not want to stop. Do not be afraid to go find kids and encourage them to go outside to have some fun. More and more children from the neighborhood will start to get involved. Everyone will begin looking forward to playing and will meet more often. Instead of sitting around inside, kids can meet one another, make friends, get exercise, and have tons of fun! This is what childhood is all about. Kids need to get back outside, exercise, and love it—and this book is the guide!

INTRODUCTION

This book is divided into five activity levels. This organization is to help you easily select a game depending on what mood the group is in and how much exercise they desire. The amount of exercise that can be expected from each game is defined below.

- **Activity Level I**: This level includes games where mostly walking or limited physical exercise is required. These games are still active and take place outside, but they are not as physically demanding as the others.
- **Activity Level II**: This level includes games where little running is required. Games may include brief periods of running with mostly stationary activity or may require less demanding physical activity.
- **Activity Level III**: This level includes games that involve running, but not constant running. There will be slows points in the game when players can rest, but everyone will still get good exercise.
- **Activity Level IV**: This level includes games that are highly active. These games are more likely to include short breaks in the action, but mostly constant movement or running are involved.

- **Activity Level V**: This level includes games that require the most exercise. These games mainly entail constant running or movement and are highly active.

I suggest searching all the activity levels to find the right game. Children who only want to run constantly and children who hate to run will all find enjoyable games within each activity level. There are fantastic games to explore throughout this book, so use it to the fullest and try them all!

A word of caution: some of the games involve physical contact and almost all require physical activity. There is some risk of injury, especially if the rules are not followed and standard safety cautions are ignored. Please be sure to follow the rules as they are stated and do not add extra physical contact. Also, please encourage the use of safety equipment when it is appropriate. Guidance and supervision are wonderful tools, especially when helping children learn a new game. Parents should help children fully understand the game and can watch to ensure that no dangerous activities are occurring. These games are highly enjoyable, but they will be even more fun if no one gets hurt!

One last thing everyone needs to know before getting started is how to pick the "It." In many of the games in this book, one or more players will need to be chosen to play a certain role, often referred to as the "It." The following section describes commonly used ways to choose this player. You can follow this guide, or players can create their own method.

PICKING THE IT

Many games require an It to be chosen and picking the It can be almost as entertaining as the game itself. It is important for players to mix up how they choose It by trying out several of these methods in different games.

First, everyone should begin in a circle. One player will then choose how It will be picked. This player controls the action. Everyone in the circle holds out one or two hands. To choose It, the controlling player will go around the circle touching everyone's hands, one at a time, while saying a chant. Certain chants have traditionally been used and several of them are listed here. The controlling player begins by tapping the hand to his or her left and then rotates clockwise around the circle. With each piece of the chant (such as one syllable, word, or phrase), the controlling player taps the next player's hand and continues around the circle until the chant ends. The controlling player must include his or her own hand in the tapping as well. When the chant ends, that last hand tapped is "landed on." If further rounds are played, the hand after the one "landed on" will be the first tapped in the next chant.

A single round can be performed where the person who is "landed on" becomes the It.

The more common and exciting way to choose It is when the person "landed on" is safe and steps out of the circle. This continues until one person is left and becomes the It.

Another way to choose It is a more elaborate version of the just-described way. Each person puts two hands in the circle. Each hand is counted, and the hand that is "landed on" is taken out. When a player's hands are both out, that player can be deemed safe or It depending on the rules the group has decided on.

I've even played a longer version where each player puts both fists in the middle. The first time a hand is landed on, it turns into a flat hand, and the next time, it is eliminated. When a player's hands are both out, that player can be deemed safe or It depending upon which rules have been selected.

Here are some favorite chants we used to choose It, but players can also make up their own.

ONE POTATO:

One potato, two potato, three potato, four.
Five potato, six potato, seven potato, more.

The hand that is touched when "more" is said is landed on.

EENY MEENY:

Eeny, meeny, miny, moe.
Catch a tiger by the toe.

If he hollers let him go.
Eeny, meeny, miny, moe.

The hand that is touched when "moe" is said the second time is landed on.

BUBBLE GUM:

Bubble gum, bubble gum, in a dish.
How many pieces do you wish?

The player landed on with "wish" says a number. That many hands are then tapped around the circle and the chant continues with a generic ending (see below). For example, if the player said "four," this could be chanted:

"1, 2, 3, 4, and you are out, you dirty old dishrag turned inside out."

Only the hand that is tapped when the last word of the generic ending is said is landed on.

ENGINE ENGINE:

Engine, engine, number nine,
Going down the Chicago line
If the train falls off the track,
Do you want your money back?

The player landed on with "back" says "yes" or "no." Then the chant continues:

Y-E-S spells yes and you shall have your money back.

or

N-O spells no and you won't have your money back.

A hand is then officially landed on at the word "back."

MY MOTHER AND YOUR MOTHER:

My mother and your mother were at the store.
Your mother punched my mother in the nose.
What color was the blood?

The player landed on names any color. The color is then spelled out and a generic ending is added. For example, if the player says "blue," then chant:

B-L-U-E spells blue and my mother told me to pick the very best one and you are It.

Only the hand that is tapped when the last word of the generic ending is said is landed on.

GENERIC ENDINGS:

And my mother told me to choose the very best one, and you are It.

And you are not It, you dirty old dishrag turned inside out.

And you are It.

CAN YOU FIND YOUR GAME?

Please look through my book for all the adventurous outdoor games you play or used to play as a child. If there are any I have forgotten, please send me an email at adventurousbook@yahoo.com with the name and a description of your game. If it fits the mold of being an exciting outdoor game, I will include it in the sequel of the book! I will also reference you in the book as the source of the game (if you desire).

ACTIVITY LEVEL I

AROUND THE WORLD

NUMBER OF KIDS: at least 2

AGES: any

TIME ALLOTTED: 30 minutes or more

PLAYING FIELD: any basketball court

EQUIPMENT: 1 basketball

START-UP: Players choose a shooting order. Everyone then determines a series of shot locations that must be made to complete a round. Usually three paths are used that require five shots each (one shot from one side, then the corner, then from straight on, then from the other corner, then the other side). The first path should be the smallest, then one a little farther away, and then one around the three-point line.

OBJECT: To get "around the world" by making every designated shot.

PLAY: The first player starts with the ball and begins the series of shots. If the first shot is made, that player immediately advances to the next shot and continues. If that player finishes one path, he or she immediately continues to the first shot in the next path. If the player should miss a shot, "chance" comes into play. If a player misses, that player can decide either to stay in place until the next turn or to take a chance. If a player takes a chance, that player shoots again. If he or she makes the shot on the chance, that player moves to the next shot and his or her turn continues. If the chance is missed, the player must restart at the very beginning at his or her next turn. Play ends when one player makes it all the way "around the world."

A second chance can be used as an optional rule. If a player missed the first chance, he or she can decide to stop and will start at the beginning in the next turn or that player can risk elimination from the game by taking a second chance. The second chance, if selected, is taken immediately after the first chance and results in automatic elimination from the game if the shot is missed. If it is made, that player moves to the next shot and his or her turn continues.

COMMENTS:

This is more competitive for experienced basketball players but can be played by anyone. The second-chance rule should only be played by beginners and if there are a lot of people. With skilled players, two chances make it too easy to go all the way around in one turn. Overall this is a good, skill-based game.

BEANBAG TOSS

NUMBER OF KIDS: at least 2

AGES: any

TIME ALLOTTED: 20 minutes or more

PLAYING FIELD: any open area

EQUIPMENT: at least 3 beanbags and the playing board. If the players do not have a playing board, parents should build or at a minimum supervise the building of the board. The playing board can be made of any large flat, rectangular board. Holes that the beanbags can fit through should be cut in the board (the number and location of holes can vary). This board can be propped up against a wall, or back legs can be built to angle it.

START-UP: Once the playing board is made and a location is found, players should assign point values to each hole in the board. A throwing line should also be marked about 20 feet away from the board. Players should determine how many points will be required to win the game or how many rounds will be played.

OBJECT: To score the highest number of points.

PLAY: Each player stands behind the throwing line and takes turns tossing the three beanbags toward the board. If a beanbag goes through a hole in the board, that player scores the corresponding number of points. Each player totals his or her points at the end of each round. The winner is the first player to reach the determined number of points. If players choose to play a certain number of rounds instead, the player with the highest total at the end of the last round is the winner.

COMMENTS:

This game was a childhood favorite of mine. Making and decorating the board can be a fun project for parents and children to do together. We used to make clown faces with holes in the eyes, nose, and mouth, but anything goes, so be creative and have fun. This is a fun, simple game that anyone can play!

BOCCE

NUMBER OF KIDS: at least 2

AGES: any

TIME ALLOTTED: 20 minutes or more

PLAYING FIELD: any large grassy area

EQUIPMENT: 1 small ball (the "bocce") and 2 or 3 slightly larger ones for each child (for example, 1 golf ball and a few tennis balls for each child)

START-UP: Players should choose the balls and find a good area to play.

OBJECT: To toss one's balls closest to the bocce.

PLAY: One player tosses the smaller "bocce" ball as far away as he or she desires. Everyone else then takes turns tossing one ball toward the bocce ball. Once everyone has tossed once, everyone tosses a second time, and so on, until all balls have been tossed. Whichever player lands one of his or her balls closest to the bocce is the winner. The winner then tosses the bocce for the next round. Play one round at a time or a series that continues until one player has five or ten wins.

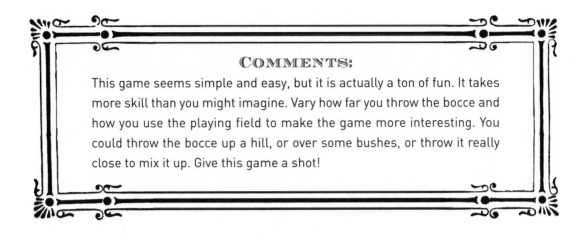

COMMENTS:

This game seems simple and easy, but it is actually a ton of fun. It takes more skill than you might imagine. Vary how far you throw the bocce and how you use the playing field to make the game more interesting. You could throw the bocce up a hill, or over some bushes, or throw it really close to mix it up. Give this game a shot!

BUILDING

NUMBER OF KIDS: 1 or more

AGES: 8 and up

TIME ALLOTTED: at least 1 hour

PLAYING FIELD: anywhere safe

EQUIPMENT: anything safe (for the child to decide with adult supervision). Outdoor materials should be the focus, such as logs or boards, but anything parents are willing to let children use, such as sheets and shovels, can also be used to help build and create.

START-UP: The players should choose what they want to build and a safe area in which to build it.

OBJECT: To find fun tools and objects to use in the creation, to experiment and learn how different structures can be created, and to continue building until satisfied with the object chosen to be built.

PLAY: Anything safe goes. Parents can help or can supervise; there are any number of different ideas of things to build, such as a dam, a fort, a tree house, etc.) The more complicated the object, the more parents should help. Builders should have fun finding materials to make the chosen object as well as tools to help them with the construction. The goal should be to make something stable or useful (perhaps to walk across, sit in, or play with). Players should take their time and try different materials and techniques until they find the best way to make their object. This can be done in a few hours or over the course of days and weeks. Players should keep trying new building ideas until the best method is discovered and they can finish and be proud of their object.

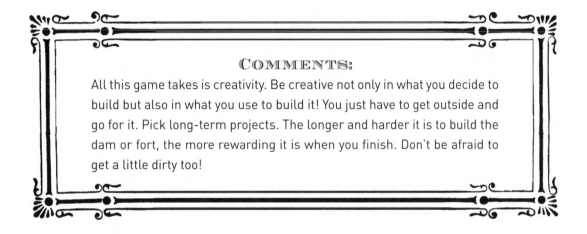

COMMENTS:

All this game takes is creativity. Be creative not only in what you decide to build but also in what you use to build it! You just have to get outside and go for it. Pick long-term projects. The longer and harder it is to build the dam or fort, the more rewarding it is when you finish. Don't be afraid to get a little dirty too!

CIRCLE TARGET BOWL

NUMBER OF KIDS: at least 2

AGES: any

TIME ALLOTTED: 30 minutes or more

PLAYING FIELD: an open strip of short grass

EQUIPMENT: something to mark 3 concentric circles and 1 or more balls to roll for each player. Lines can be made with string or rope. If these are not available, the game can be played with three concentric squares using cones or any objects to mark the corners.

START-UP: Players should mark off three or more concentric circles (or squares) and assign a point value to each. The values should be assigned by giving the innermost circle the highest value, with values decreasing toward the outside circle. Players then designate a starting line that is a reasonable distance from the circles and can choose teams if desired.

OBJECT: To score the most points.

PLAY: Each player stands behind the starting line and takes turns rolling his or her ball(s) toward the circles. Each player must roll from behind the starting line. After all the balls have been rolled, the players or teams tally up the points they have earned. The winner can be the first to reach a set number of points or whoever has the highest total after ten rounds.

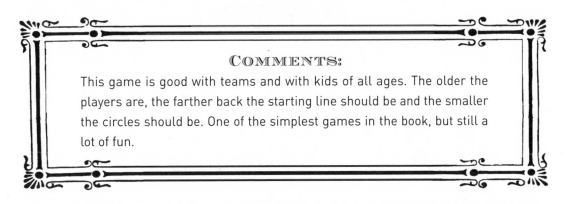

COMMENTS:

This game is good with teams and with kids of all ages. The older the players are, the farther back the starting line should be and the smaller the circles should be. One of the simplest games in the book, but still a lot of fun.

Variant:

MULTIPLE TARGET THROW: This game is played by throwing objects (player's choice) instead of rolling. Players can use concentric circles, one lone target, or multiple targets. If multiple targets are used, targets should be close to one another and the smaller targets worth more points. Targets can also be moved around the playing field between rounds and/or the objects tossed can be changed to keep the game interesting, if desired.

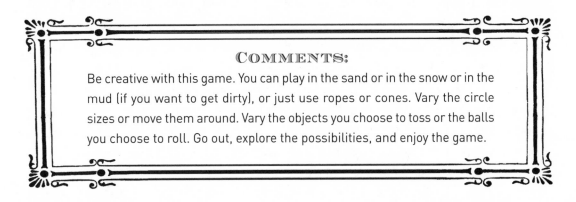

COMMENTS:

Be creative with this game. You can play in the sand or in the snow or in the mud (if you want to get dirty), or just use ropes or cones. Vary the circle sizes or move them around. Vary the objects you choose to toss or the balls you choose to roll. Go out, explore the possibilities, and enjoy the game.

CORN TOSS

NUMBER OF KIDS: 2 teams of 2 players

AGES: any

TIME ALLOTTED: 40 minutes or more

PLAYING FIELD: any long, open area

EQUIPMENT: 2 matching sets of 4 beanbags (8 beanbags total). 2 slightly slanted beanbag boards. These can be made using thin plywood. The boards should be about 2 feet wide, 4 feet long, and the back end raised about 1 foot. They should only have 1 hole in the middle upper part of the board, big enough for the beanbag to fall through. If the players do not have a playing board, parents can buy or build the boards or at a minimum supervise the building of the boards.

START-UP: Players should spread the two boards about 20 feet apart. Teams play from opposite sides of the field. This will result in your partner standing at the opposite board and one opponent standing at your board and one opponent standing with your partner. The opponents on one side of the field start with all eight beanbags - one set going to each player.

OBJECT: To score 21 points first.

PLAY: The players with the beanbags take turns tossing one beanbag toward the opposite board until all bags are tossed. Players are not allowed to cross the front of their board while tossing. At the end of the first round, one point is awarded for each beanbag that is on top of the board, and three points are awarded for each bag that fell through the hole. Here is the tricky part: only the difference in score is kept (so if team A scores eight points and team B scores five points, team A gets three points for that round and team B gets zero points). After the final points are tallied, the other two players then toss the bags in the same fashion. The team that has most recently gained points throws the first bag. The game ends when 21 points are reached.

COMMENTS:

This game is slightly more complicated than a regular beanbag toss, but it is much more fun for older kids and even parents. It takes a lot of skill. Play for a while to improve your game. Close competition makes the game even more fun!

DEAD BOX

NUMBER OF KIDS: at least 2

AGES: any

TIME ALLOTTED: 45 minutes or more

PLAYING FIELD: a safe area of pavement or cement that can be drawn on with chalk

EQUIPMENT: chalk and 1 metal or plastic bottle cap for each player. Pebbles, balls of tin foil, or anything fun and easy to toss can be used if bottle caps are not available.

START-UP: One player should draw a large box on the ground with the chalk. The large box can vary in size, but approximately five feet by five feet is recommended. Within the box, twelve smaller boxes along the inside edge should be drawn (one in each corner and two between the corner boxes along each side). The boxes should be numbered 1 through 12 starting anywhere. Then a skull and crossbones, or an *X*, or the words *dead box* are drawn inside the remaining inner square. Examples are shown on page 24. Players should mark a throwing spot on the ground a reasonable distance away from the square and choose a throwing order. The size of the squares and dead box, as well as the distance of the throwing spot should be varied depending on the skill of the players. Better, more experienced players should draw smaller boxes and/or a more distant throwing spot. Multiple throwing spots may also be used in the same game if beginning or younger players are going against older or more experienced players.

OBJECT: To be the first to successfully complete the entire round.

PLAY: The first player stands or sits on the throwing spot and attempts to flick his or her bottle cap into the box marked 1. All throws are made from the marked spot. If the player successfully lands the bottle cap in the box, he or she goes again, this time shooting for box 2, then box 3, and so on. As soon as the player misses a box, his or her turn is over and the next person takes his or her turn. On their next turn, players resume shooting for the box that they missed on the previous turn. If a bottle cap lands in the "dead box," however, then that player's turn ends and the player must begin back at box 1 on the next turn. The winner is the first to finish the round by landing his or her bottle cap successfully in box 12.

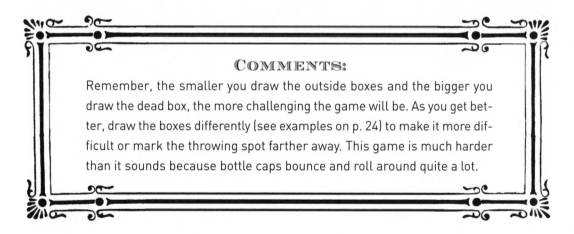

COMMENTS:

Remember, the smaller you draw the outside boxes and the bigger you draw the dead box, the more challenging the game will be. As you get better, draw the boxes differently (see examples on p. 24) to make it more difficult or mark the throwing spot farther away. This game is much harder than it sounds because bottle caps bounce and roll around quite a lot.

The diagram below shows the standard box design that should be used by beginners.

1	2	3	4
12	DEAD		5
11	BOX		6
10	9	8	7

The diagram below shows an example of a more complex box design that should be can be used by more advanced players.

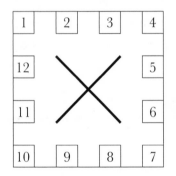

DOWN, DOWN, DOWN

NUMBER OF KIDS: at least 2

AGES: any

TIME ALLOTTED: 20 minutes or more

PLAYING FIELD: any open area of grass

EQUIPMENT: 1 tennis ball

START-UP: Players should spread out evenly in a circle so they can toss the ball to one another.

OBJECT: To be the last person remaining.

PLAY: One player starts with the ball and throws it to the player on their left. If a successful catch is made, there is no penalty and the catcher then throws the ball to the next person on his or her left, and so on. Penalties occur when a ball is dropped (penalty to the catcher) or thrown so poorly that it cannot be caught (penalty to the thrower). When a player incurs his or her first penalty, everyone says together, "Down on one knee." That player must then get down on one knee and continue playing from that position. The second penalty is "Down on two knees," and then "Down on one elbow." The fourth penalty means elimination from the game. Each time a player incurs a penalty, that player must continue to catch and pass as before, but he or she must do so in the said position, which makes it more and more difficult. When a player is eliminated, players remain exactly where they are and play continues. This continues until only one player is left.

An alternate rule can be used where the player with the ball may throw it to anyone he or she chooses, instead of having to throw it to the player to his or her left.

COMMENTS:

This game can be a blast to watch and to play. It is harder but more fun to be down on your knees or knees and one elbow. This is good catching and throwing practice and is very challenging and fun!

FRISBEE GOLF

NUMBER OF KIDS: 1 or 2 or more for competition

AGES: any

TIME ALLOTTED: 30 minutes or more

PLAYING FIELD: a large, fairly open area, such as a yard, several adjacent yards, or a field

EQUIPMENT: 1 Frisbee for each child

START-UP: Players should choose a Frisbee and find a starting point. They should then choose how many holes are going to be played, or they can choose to simply play one hole at a time until they wish to stop.

OBJECT: To hit the chosen target in the fewest number of throws.

PLAY: One player chooses an object, such as a tree trunk, as the goal for the first hole. As in golf, players then take turns throwing their Frisbees toward the destination. Each player tries to hit the target in the fewest number of throws. Once each player has reached the destination, the winner of the hole chooses the next target. Turns may also be taken to choose the next hole. The winner, as in regular golf, is the player who takes the fewest total throws or wins the most individual holes.

COMMENTS:

I highly recommend this game. It's tons of fun and can be played any-where by anyone. Make long holes by choosing targets that are far away and launch the Frisbee hard!

Variant:

SOCCER GOLF: In this game, players follow the same rules but kick a soccer ball instead of throwing a Frisbee.

HOME RUN DERBY

NUMBER OF KIDS: at least 3

AGES: 8 and up

TIME ALLOTTED: 30 minutes or more

PLAYING FIELD: any large, open area

EQUIPMENT: 1 baseball bat and 1 or more balls to hit (can be baseballs in a baseball field or tennis balls for more urban areas) and 1 baseball mitt for each player

START-UP: Players should find a large area in which to play and choose a home run line. The home run line represents the distance the ball must travel to achieve a home run. Thus home runs are not scored by running bases, but by hitting the ball over the home run line. The batting order, then number of rounds, and the number of outs a player is allowed to receive (usually three, five, or ten) before his or her turn is over must be selected.

OBJECT: To hit the most home runs.

PLAY: One person chooses to bat first and one person chooses to pitch. Everyone else spreads around the field to help retrieve balls. When everyone is ready, the pitcher throws the first pitch to the batter. The pitches must be slow and easy to hit, perhaps thrown underhand. If the batter hits a home run on that pitch, the batter begins to count his or her home run total. If the batter hits anything other than a home run, he or she receives one out. That batter hits until he or she receives the chosen number of outs. The next batter then steps up, and someone else can step in as pitcher too. Each batter should remember how many home runs he or she hit during the round. After everyone has had a chance to bat, the round ends. Players can hit as many rounds as they want, and the winner is the person who has the highest tally of home runs.

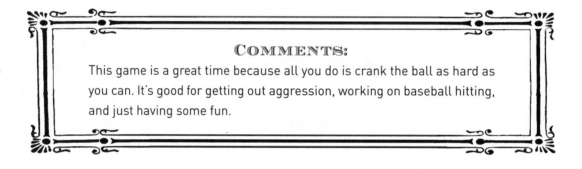

COMMENTS:

This game is a great time because all you do is crank the ball as hard as you can. It's good for getting out aggression, working on baseball hitting, and just having some fun.

HORSE

NUMBER OF KIDS: at least 2

AGES: any

TIME ALLOTTED: 25 minutes or more

PLAYING FIELD: any basketball court

EQUIPMENT: 1 basketball

START-UP: Players find an area to play and choose a shooting order.

OBJECT: To be the last player remaining.

PLAY: The first player starts with the basketball and can shoot any type of shot from any place on the court. If the player misses the shot, it becomes the next person's turn to shoot any shot of his of her choice from any location. The only exception is that the same person should not shoot from the same place where he or she made a previous shot. If a player makes his or her shot, the next person in line must then make the same shot. If the second player matches that shot, the third player must make the shot, and so on. If everyone matches the shot, the original shooter loses his or her turn. If anyone who is trying to match a shot misses, he or she earns a letter. The first letter a player earns is *H*, then *O*, then *R*, then *S*, and finally *E*. Once a player has earned *H-O-R-S-E*, that player is out of the game.

Once a player earns a letter, the original shot no longer has to be matched, and the next person in line shoots a new shot (for example, if player 1 makes a shot and player 2 fails to match the shot, player 2 earns a letter and then player 3 shoots from anywhere). Some people play that everyone must try to match the shot, but the way described here is more common. Play continues until everyone but one player has spelled "Horse." This last player is the winner.

COMMENTS:
This game helps work on basketball skills and is fun and competitive. Be creative with your shots and go for some crazy ones; it can be even more fun that way.

JACKS

NUMBER OF KIDS: at least 2

AGES: any

TIME ALLOTTED: 20 minutes or more

PLAYING FIELD: a porch or a small cement or paved area

EQUIPMENT: 1 small bouncy ball and 10 jacks (these can be cheaply bought or any small, easily scoopable objects can be substituted)

START-UP: Players should find an area to play and determine the order that players will take their turn.

OBJECT: To pick up the most jacks in each round.

PLAY: The first player spreads the 10 jacks out in a small area on the ground. That player then drops the bouncy ball. The same player then picks up one jack and catches the ball before it bounces more than once. If he or she fails to do this, the turn is over. If successful, the player repeats the process picking up one jack at a time until all 10 jacks have been picked up. If successful, the player spreads the 10 jacks out in the small area again and repeats the process, this time picking up two jacks at a time. If successful, the player repeats the process picking up 3 jacks at a time (there will be 1 left over which also needs to be picked up in the same fashion), and so on up to picking up all 10 jacks at a time. On every attempt, the ball can only bounce once and the correct number of jacks must be scooped up, otherwise the player's turn is over. The next player then takes his or her turn, starting at one jack at a time. On a player's second turn, he or she must start over at one jack at a time. Several rounds are played, and the winner is the person who got up to the highest number of jacks in one turn.

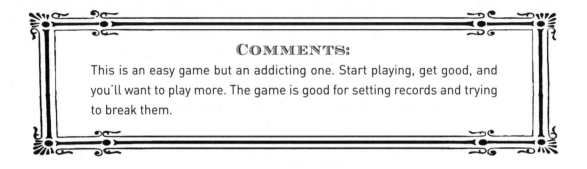

COMMENTS:

This is an easy game but an addicting one. Start playing, get good, and you'll want to play more. The game is good for setting records and trying to break them.

LAWN DARTS

NUMBER OF KIDS: at least 2

AGES: any

TIME ALLOTTED: 30 minutes or more

PLAYING FIELD: an open strip of grass

EQUIPMENT: 2 hoops (hula-hoop size) and 3 to 5 lawn darts. Lawn darts can be bought or a number of other objects can be substituted for them (like sticks or balls, or even old shoes).

START-UP: Players should spread the hoops out a reasonable distance and set them on the ground. If there are more than two players, teams should be formed. Each player or team then stands behind a hoop. Players should choose how many points are required for the game to be won (usually ten, fifteen, or twenty).

OBJECT: To score the most points.

PLAY: One player or team starts with all the lawn darts and tosses them toward the opponents' hoop. A player must toss from behind his or her own hoop. After all the darts have been tossed, one point is awarded for each dart that lands inside the hoop. The opposing team then tosses the darts in the same fashion. The winner is the first to reach the selected number of points.

If enough darts are present (so each team has a matching set of 3 to 5 darts), an alternative set of rules can be put in place. Each team throws its darts at the same time. A team then scores by making a greater number of darts than its opponent. For example, if during the first round of tossing, team 1 successfully lands all five darts in team 2's hoop, and team 2 only lands two darts, then team 1 scores the difference of three points. Play also goes until one team reaches the chosen number of points.

COMMENTS:

This game is easy and tons of fun. Anyone can play. It takes some practice and gets more fun as you improve. Develop your own style of throwing and go for it!

LAWN GOLF

NUMBER OF KIDS: 1, or 2 or more for competition

AGES: 8 and up

TIME ALLOTTED: 30 minutes or more

PLAYING FIELD: a large, fairly open area, such as a large yard, several adjacent yards, or a field

EQUIPMENT: 1 golf club and 1 tennis ball for each player

START-UP: Players should choose a golf club, grab a tennis ball, and find a starting point. They should then choose how many holes are going to be played, or they can choose to simply play one hole at a time until they wish to stop.

OBJECT: To hit the chosen target(s) in the fewest number of strokes.

PLAY: One player chooses an object, such as a tree, as the target for the first hole. As in real golf, the players then take turns hitting their balls toward the destination. Each player tries to hit the target in the fewest number of strokes. Once each player has reached the destination, the winner of the hole (the player with the fewest strokes) chooses the next target. Players may also take turns choosing the next hole, especially if a tie occurs. A course of a predetermined number of holes may be played, or participants can simply play hole by hole. The winner, as in regular golf, is the player who takes the fewest total strokes or wins the most individual holes.

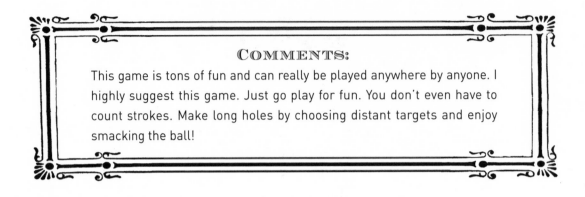

COMMENTS:

This game is tons of fun and can really be played anywhere by anyone. I highly suggest this game. Just go play for fun. You don't even have to count strokes. Make long holes by choosing distant targets and enjoy smacking the ball!

LINE CLUB BOWL

NUMBER OF KIDS: at least 2

AGES: any

TIME ALLOTTED: 40 minutes or more

PLAYING FIELD: an open strip of short grass

EQUIPMENT: 3 pins and 1 ball of choice per player or team. Pins can be anything that could topple over like bowling pins, such as small cones, tennis ball cans, or even large plastic cups.

START-UP: Players should determine a starting line and set up the pins in a triangular pattern a reasonable distance from the line. Players then choose an order to bowl and how many throws each player will get (ten is recommended).

OBJECT: To have the highest score after ten rounds or to reach a certain score first.

PLAY: Players take turns bowling from behind the starting line. The first player takes all of his or her throws before the next player has a turn. For each throw, one point is scored for knocking down a pin, three points are scored for knocking down two pins, and five points are scored for knocking down all three pins in one throw. Players continue to take turns bowling and keep track of their own scores. A twist is that if a player only knocks down one pin, it stays down for every throw until all three pins are knocked down. Pins are then set back up. The winner is the player who has the most points.

An alternative method is players can see how many throws it takes to earn a certain number of points (chosen before the game begins). The winner is the player who earns that number of points in the smallest number of throws.

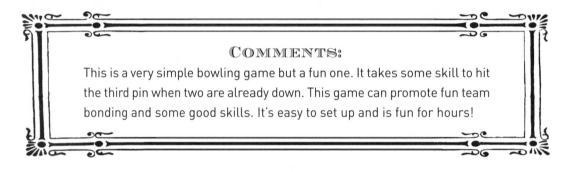

COMMENTS:

This is a very simple bowling game but a fun one. It takes some skill to hit the third pin when two are already down. This game can promote fun team bonding and some good skills. It's easy to set up and is fun for hours!

Variant:

STAKE TARGET BOWL: In this game, one stake is put into the ground. Each bowler has several balls. Players take turns rolling from behind the predetermined line. One point is awarded for each time a ball hits the stake. The winner is the player who has the most points at the end of ten throws. Sudden death is played if players are tied after 10 throws.

LONG BALL

Number of kids: at least 5

Ages: 8 and up

Time allotted: 30 minutes or more

Playing field: any large, open area

Equipment: 1 baseball bat and 1 or more balls to hit (can be baseballs in a baseball field or tennis balls in more urban areas) and 1 baseball mitt for each child

Start-up: Players should find a big area in which to play and choose one or more bases (usually just one but can be two or three). Players then decide how many outs each batter can get before his or her turn ends (usually three, five, or ten) and how many turns at bat each player will have.

Object: To hit the most home runs.

Play: One person chooses to bat first and one person chooses to pitch. One player should be a catcher as well. Everyone else spreads around the field. When everyone is ready, the pitcher throws the first pitch to the batter. The pitches must be slow and easy to hit. If the batter hits the ball, he or she must run to the base(s) chosen and make it home safely without being tagged out or forced out at home. If successful, the batter earns one home run. Otherwise, any other hit (foul ball, caught fly, tag out, force out, etc.) results in one out. That batter hits until he or she receives the selected number of outs. The next batter then steps up, and someone else can take a turn as pitcher. Each player should remember how many runs they have hit. After everyone has had a chance to bat, the round ends. Players bat the chosen number of rounds, and the winner is the person who has the highest tally of home runs.

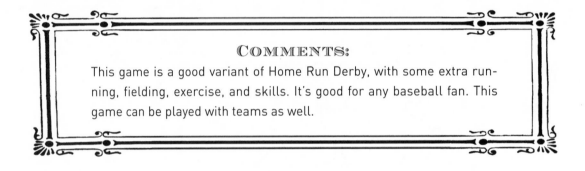

COMMENTS:

This game is a good variant of Home Run Derby, with some extra running, fielding, exercise, and skills. It's good for any baseball fan. This game can be played with teams as well.

MARBLES

NUMBER OF KIDS: at least 2

AGES: any

TIME ALLOTTED: 20 minutes or more

PLAYING FIELD: a small, rough-surfaced area, such as bare ground with packed dirt or sand

---

EQUIPMENT: 1 "shooter" (large marble) and the desired number of small marbles for each child

START-UP: Players should draw a circle on the ground, roughly 18 inches in diameter, to designate the playing area. They then spread out their marbles randomly within the circle.

OBJECT: To knock the most marbles out of the circle.

PLAY: Each player takes turns shooting his or her "shooter" into the circle in an attempt to knock small marbles out of the circle. This is done by sticking the marble on top of the hand and flicking it with the thumb. The player's hand must stay out of the circle while shooting. Any marble successfully knocked out goes into that player's pile. Once all the marbles are shot out of the circle, the player with the largest pile wins.

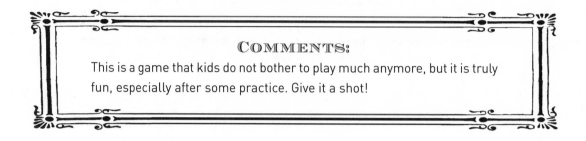

COMMENTS:

This is a game that kids do not bother to play much anymore, but it is truly fun, especially after some practice. Give it a shot!

MOTHER, MAY I?

NUMBER OF KIDS: at least 3

AGES: any

TIME ALLOTTED: 20 minutes or more

PLAYING FIELD: a long path on any surface

EQUIPMENT: none

START-UP: Players should designate a playing area and choose one person to be the "mother." The mother stands at one end of the playing area and everyone else stands together at the other end. The mother turns his or her back toward the players.

OBJECT: To be the first player to reach the end where the mother is standing.

PLAY: Each player take turns asking permission from the mother to move forward. They phrase questions in the form, "Mother, may I … ?" and request to take any number of baby steps, regular steps, big steps, leaps, and so on. For example, a player asks, "Mother, may I take two big steps?" The mother then says yes or no. If a request is granted, that player moves forward accordingly. If a request is denied, the player must take one step backward. The first player to reach the mother is then the mother for the next round.

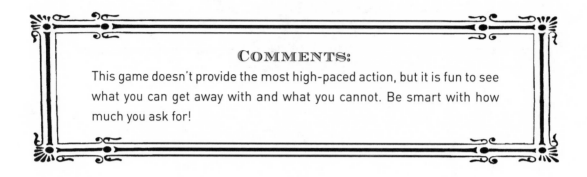

COMMENTS:

This game doesn't provide the most high-paced action, but it is fun to see what you can get away with and what you cannot. Be smart with how much you ask for!

PAPER PLANE CONTEST

NUMBER OF KIDS: at least 2

AGES: any

TIME ALLOTTED: at least 20 minutes

PLAYING FIELD: any open area

EQUIPMENT: a few sheets of paper for each child

START-UP: Everyone should have some semifirm paper to use (for example, computer paper works well). Players select how many planes they can build and how many they can enter into the contest. For examples, all players could build 5 planes and have to pick their favorite two (after trying them out) to enter into the contest. They should also select how many throws with each plane they will take.

OBJECT: To build a plane that will fly the farthest.

PLAY: As long as players use only one sheet of paper per plane, they can fold that sheet in any way they please. Once all the planes are constructed and selected, players should find a starting line and take turns throwing their planes. Players take the chosen number of throws with each plane and use an object to mark their longest throw. The winner is the person who had the plane that flew the farthest. Fold new planes or keep old ones and try it again!

COMMENTS:

This is a very simple game, but it can be a lot of fun, especially for younger kids or kids who love paper airplanes. You can keep the best planes to fly in multiple contests or start over each time. Be creative and try different folding techniques to see if you can beat your best record.

POTSY

NUMBER OF KIDS: at least 2

AGES: any

TIME ALLOTTED: 30 minutes or more

PLAYING FIELD: a large paved area that can be drawn on with chalk

---

EQUIPMENT: 1 piece of chalk, 1 ball that bounces well, and 1 small rock to toss

START-UP: A ball that bounces should be selected, such as a racquetball or playground ball. All players should use the same ball for each game, but once a new game begins a different ball can be tried. Part of the fun is trying out different types of balls.

One player should draw ten squares along the ground (about two feet wide each) and write the name of a different category in each square. Categories should be familiar to all players, such as states, vegetables, and animals. Each player should find a rock to toss and the players should decide on a throwing order. A throwing line should also be marked about five feet back from the boxes.

OBJECT: To finish the course first.

PLAY: The first player stands on the throwing line and tosses his or her rock into the first square. If successful, that player attempts to "run the course." Running the course is done by bouncing the ball and catching it once in each square. As this is done, the player must say aloud a member of the category that is written in the box where the ball is bouncing. For examples, if box one says "animal" and box two says "food," the player would first have to stand on the throwing line and toss his or her pebble into the "animal" box. If successful, he or she would bounce the ball in the animal box and say "skunk" before catching the ball. If successful, the player would then attempt to toss his or her pebble into the "food" box. If successful, he or she would have to bounce the ball into the animal box again and say a different animal, such as "giraffe," then bounce the ball in the "food" box and say a food, such as "pizza," before catching it. This would continue until the player went up to the tenth box or made an error and lost his or her turn. A player's turn ends when the rock is not tossed into the correct box or the course is not completed correctly. Course errors include dropping the ball, bouncing it on a line or in the wrong box, or failing to name a correct member of a category before catching the ball. On each subsequent turn, a player begins where he or she made an error on the last turn. The first player to make it through all ten boxes is the winner.

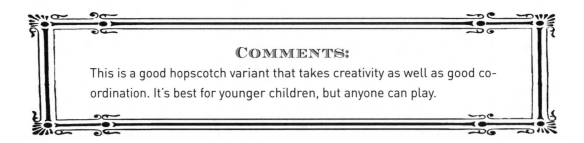

COMMENTS:
This is a good hopscotch variant that takes creativity as well as good co-ordination. It's best for younger children, but anyone can play.

REARS UP

NUMBER OF KIDS: at least 3

AGES: 10 and up

TIME ALLOTTED: 20 minutes or more

PLAYING FIELD: a small area of any surface

EQUIPMENT: 1 soccer ball or footbag

START-UP: One person starts with the ball and everyone gets into a circle.

OBJECT: To avoid receiving letters.

PLAY: The player who has the ball begins to juggle it (hitting it into the air and keeping it there). Hands and arms are never allowed to be used, but use of any other body part is fine. The person who starts the ball in the air may immediately knock it over to someone else or juggle it a few times him- or herself. There is no limit to how many consecutive times a player can juggle the ball. The ball continues to be passed from person to person in the air until a player causes the ball to drop to the ground. This can happen if a player drops a pass that came to him or her or if someone's pass is unplayable. If a player causes the ball to drop, that player gains one letter. Players are always responsible for playing the ball if it comes close to them. Failure to do so also results in a letter. A player earns an *R* the first time he or she causes the ball to drop, then an *E*, and so on, until *R-E-A-R-S* is spelled. The first person to spell the word is eliminated.

The game may end there and players can start over, or older players can play the following rule: the eliminated player turns around and places his or her hands on a wall. The rest of the players take one turn either throwing or kicking the ball at this player (depending on what type of ball was used). Then a new round begins. Each new round, everyone starts with no letters.

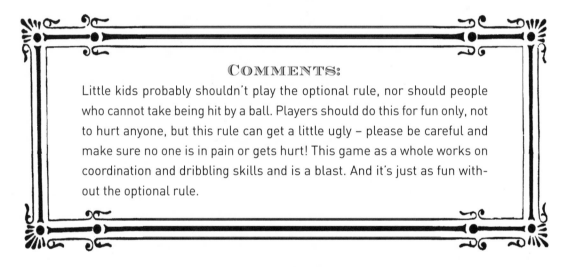

COMMENTS:

Little kids probably shouldn't play the optional rule, nor should people who cannot take being hit by a ball. Players should do this for fun only, not to hurt anyone, but this rule can get a little ugly – please be careful and make sure no one is in pain or gets hurt! This game as a whole works on coordination and dribbling skills and is a blast. And it's just as fun without the optional rule.

SOCCER CROQUET

NUMBER OF KIDS: 2 or more

AGES: any

TIME ALLOTTED: 20 minutes or more

PLAYING FIELD: a small grassy area

EQUIPMENT: 1 soccer ball for each player and several plastic cones (or something similar such as large plastic cups or even shoes)

START-UP: Players make a croquet course using cones. This is done by setting up a series of cones in the grassy area. The cones should be set in pairs about two feet apart, so that a soccer ball can be easily kicked between them. The pairs can be spread around the course in any manner. Players should choose an order of play. A beginning point should also be designated.

OBJECT: To be the first player to finish the course.

PLAY: The first player sets his or her ball at the beginning point. The player then attempts to kick the ball through the first pair of cones. If successful, this player then kicks toward the second pair of cones, and so forth. Kicking the ball through the cones in the wrong direction does not count. As soon as a player fails to kick the ball through the next pair of cones, that player's turn is finished. The next player then starts at the beginning point and proceeds in the same way. At the end of a player's turn, his or her ball remains where it is, to be kicked again from that point in the next round. Players must finish the course, turn around, and then come back through it in the reverse direction. The winner is the first player to return to the beginning point. If one player's ball hits another player's ball, the balls are simply played from where they lie after the collision.

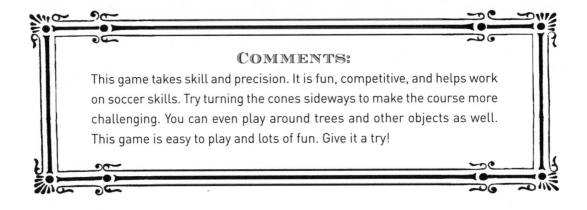

COMMENTS:

This game takes skill and precision. It is fun, competitive, and helps work on soccer skills. Try turning the cones sideways to make the course more challenging. You can even play around trees and other objects as well. This game is easy to play and lots of fun. Give it a try!

THROW FOR DISTANCE

NUMBER OF KIDS: at least 2

AGES: any

TIME ALLOTTED: 20 minutes or more

PLAYING FIELD: a long, open area of grass or field

EQUIPMENT: an equal number of chosen throwing objects for each player (usually balls of any kind, but other safe objects such as Frisbees can also be used)

START-UP: Players should select all the objects to be thrown (for example, two tennis balls, two different-sized footballs, one soccer ball, three Frisbees, and one lawn dart per player). Then a throwing line is chosen and all the objects are set behind the line. The players then mark off lines at any distance down the field. Throwing past the first line will be worth one point, past the second is worth two points, and so on. Usually five lines are drawn, but this can vary.

OBJECT: To score the most points.

PLAY: Play begins with the players standing behind the throwing line. The players then take turns throwing an object as far as they can. Each then throws the next object and so on until all objects have been thrown. Players can agree on one or more throwing attempts with hard-to-throw objects, such as Frisbees. All the points earned by each player are added up and the player with the most points wins.

COMMENTS:

This game is extremely fun and simple. Try all sorts of balls. You'll be surprised how much variance there can be in who throws best with different objects. Try this out and let 'em rip!

UNTANGLE

NUMBER OF KIDS: at least 5

AGES: any

TIME ALLOTTED: 20 minutes or more

PLAYING FIELD: a small, open area of grass or soft surface

EQUIPMENT: none

START-UP: Everyone gets into a circle. Each player then simultaneously reaches into the circle and randomly grabs one hand of two different people.

OBJECT: To untangle the mess that has just been formed.

PLAY: In this game, anything goes—except players cannot let go of the hands they are holding, not even for a second! Players may do anything else to attempt to return eventually to an untangled circle in which no one's arms are crossed. This is a group goal and everyone wins!

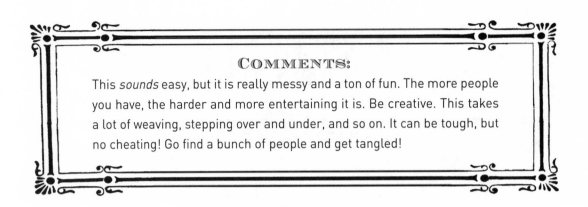

COMMENTS:

This *sounds* easy, but it is really messy and a ton of fun. The more people you have, the harder and more entertaining it is. Be creative. This takes a lot of weaving, stepping over and under, and so on. It can be tough, but no cheating! Go find a bunch of people and get tangled!

WATER BALLOON TOSS

NUMBER OF KIDS: at least 2 teams of 2

AGES: any

TIME ALLOTTED: 10 minutes or more

PLAYING FIELD: a yard or open grass area

EQUIPMENT: 1 water balloon per team for each game played

START-UP: Players should pair off into teams and each team gets one water balloon. Opponents get in two side-by-side lines, with teammates facing each other.

OBJECT: To be the only remaining team with an unpopped balloon.

PLAY: Everyone on one side starts with the water balloon. Each player then passes the balloon to his or her teammate. If the balloon did not pop, whoever just passed the balloon takes a big step back. The balloon is then tossed back, and the thrower again takes a step back. Each team must pass and step back in unison to ensure that each team stays the same distance apart. If a team's balloon breaks at any time, the team is out of the game. The winner is proclaimed when there is only one remaining team with an unpopped balloon. Players can switch or keep partners and try it again as many times as desired.

COMMENTS:

This game is good for a really hot day. You'll get a little wet and have some great competition and fun!

 # ACTIVITY LEVEL II

500

NUMBER OF KIDS: at least 4

AGES: any

TIME ALLOTTED: 20 minutes or more

PLAYING FIELD: a long strip of grass or pavement

EQUIPMENT: 1 soft football (other types of balls may be substituted, but footballs are best)

START-UP: Players should select a ball and choose one person to be the thrower.

OBJECT: To become the thrower by earning 500 points.

PLAY: The thrower lines up away from everyone else roughly the distance he or she can easily toss the football. Everyone else stands near one another. When everyone is ready, the thrower chooses a number of points, for example, 200. The thrower then yells this number to everyone and at the same time throws the ball into the air. The ball should land somewhere among the group of catchers. If a player catches the ball, he or she earns the number of points called by the thrower. In this example, the catcher would get 200 points for catching the ball in the air. A generally accepted option is to award half the points for catching the ball after one bounce (so 100 points would be earned on a 200-point throw if the ball bounced one time). If no one catches the ball, no points are earned. Either way, the ball is then returned to the thrower, who again calls out a number while throwing the football. Once a catcher reaches a point total of 500 or more, that player then becomes the thrower and another round begins. Every time a new player becomes the thrower, everyone's point total is reset to zero. Play ends when the players no longer wish to play.

OPTIONS: Two other calls exist if the thrower desires. "Jackpot" may be called, meaning an automatic token to 500 for anyone who catches the ball (only applies if caught in the air). "Mystery" may also be called, where only the thrower knows the value of the toss until it is caught (one bounce is still acceptable for half points here, unless of course the mystery is a Jackpot).

COMMENTS:

This is a fun game that anyone can play. The trick is to vary the throwing: throw some high, some low, some a little off to the side, some very far or short. Mix up the calls too, and don't be too stingy. Be aggressive in catching as well, but be careful not to mow over smaller players!

ATTACK

NUMBER OF KIDS: 2 teams of at least 3

AGES: 8 and up

TIME ALLOTTED: 20 minutes or more

PLAYING FIELD: any open, grassy area

EQUIPMENT: none. Two hats or objects that can be placed on one's head may be needed if a certain attack is chosen.

START-UP: Players should split into two teams and define a circular area to be the region of attack. The circle includes a line across the middle, called the "pull line." Each team chooses a captain. The number of attack wins required to end the game should also be determined.

OBJECT: To be the first to win the selected number of attacks.

PLAY: One captain chooses a player from each team to "attack" in the circle. The other captain then chooses the method of the attack (see the next page). The two chosen players enter the circle, perform the chosen method of attack, and a point is given to the winner. This process repeats after each attack, but the captains alternate jobs. This goes until one team has reached the selected number of wins.

Methods of attack include but are not limited to the following:

1. Players grasp right hands (or left hands) over the pull line and try to pull opponent over the line.
2. Players link right elbows (or left elbows) over the pull line and try to pull opponent over the line.
3. Players try to break through the opponent's line first. The players of the two teams join hands standing on their own side of the circle. The attackers start in the middle of the circle and one captain yells "Go!" The attackers then try to be the first to break through their opponent's line, similar to Red Rover.
4. Players fold their arms across their chest and push the opponent out of the combat circle. No other players are involved.
5. Players hop on one foot, holding the other foot behind the body in one hand, and with the other arm across the chest and grasping the opposite shoulder, cause opponent to replace his or her foot to the floor or fall over.
6. One player runs to a chosen spot before the opponent tags him or her (a slight lead is given to the runner–for example, each can start on one side of the circle). The chosen spot can be any object outside of the circle and should be about 40–50 feet away.
7. Players try to be the first to knock off or steal the opponent's hat (or other object that can placed on one's head) without stepping outside the circle.
8. Players try to be the first to snatch the opponent's tail without stepping outside the circle. For this, a handkerchief or cloth band is placed under the back of each player's belt or waistline.

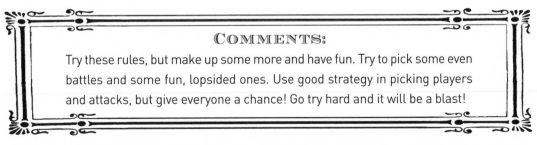

COMMENTS:

Try these rules, but make up some more and have fun. Try to pick some even battles and some fun, lopsided ones. Use good strategy in picking players and attacks, but give everyone a chance! Go try hard and it will be a blast!

BUCK, BUCK

NUMBER OF KIDS: 2 teams of at least 4

AGES: 8 and up

TIME ALLOTTED: 20 minutes or more

PLAYING FIELD: an open, grassy area

EQUIPMENT: none

START-UP: Players should find an open place to play and choose teams. One team decides to be the "buck" and the other team's members are the "jumpers." One player on the buck's team stands up straight and is called the "post." Another player on the buck's team then bends over and braces him- or herself against the post by wrapping his or her arms around the waist of the post. The rest of the buck team continues this, each bending over and wrapping his or her arms around the player's waist in front of them to form the buck. The post should be facing the same direction as the rest of his or her team. The jumpers all stand about ten feet behind the end of the buck.

OBJECT: To collapse the buck.

PLAY: The first jumper holds up one, two, or three fingers and yells, "Buck, buck, how many fingers do I hold up?" The post cannot look and must guess one, two, or three. If the post is correct, that jumper's turn is over and the next jumper does the same. If the post is wrong, the jumper replies, "Three you say, and two there be" (substitute the appropriate numbers). The jumper is then allowed to run and leap (from behind) onto the buck. The jumper must leap from behind the bent-over players (the buck) in a leapfrog fashion and will land on top of the other players and must try to stay on. The jumper should leap as far as he or she can (over as many of the bent-over players as possible) to allow room for others. A jumper should land by straddling the buck, as one would sit on a horse. If the buck collapses, the round is over and the teams switch. If not, the jumper stays on top of the buck where he or she landed and the next jumper then repeats the process, starting with yelling, "Buck, buck, how many fingers do I hold up?"

During a round, jumpers try to collapse the buck. If successful, the jumpers earn one point, and if unsuccessful, the buck earns one point for each unsuccessful jumper. For example, if two players have jumped and landed on the buck, then the third player that jumps on collapses it, the team that is the buck would receive two points for holding up two jumpers and the jumping team would receive one point when the third jumper collapsed the buck. The teams then switch and the process repeats. The winner is the team that accumulates the most points at the end of several rounds.

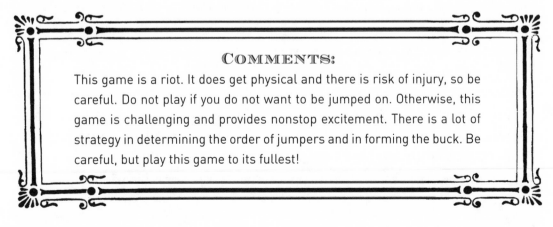

COMMENTS:

This game is a riot. It does get physical and there is risk of injury, so be careful. Do not play if you do not want to be jumped on. Otherwise, this game is challenging and provides nonstop excitement. There is a lot of strategy in determining the order of jumpers and in forming the buck. Be careful, but play this game to its fullest!

CROSSING THE BROOK

NUMBER OF KIDS: at least 2

AGES: any

TIME ALLOTTED: 5 minutes or more

PLAYING FIELD: any open, grassy area

EQUIPMENT: 2 objects to mark the ends of the brook (like broomsticks or pieces of rope)

START-UP: Place the two chosen objects a few feet apart.

OBJECT: To be the last remaining player.

PLAY: Players take turns attempting to jump over the brook. Each player who does not successfully jump all the way across the brook is eliminated from the game. After each player has jumped, the brook is widened and the remaining players must jump over it again. At the beginning of each round, the brook is widened until only one player successfully jumps over it. This player is the winner.

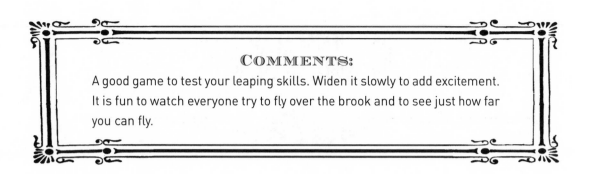

COMMENTS:

A good game to test your leaping skills. Widen it slowly to add excitement. It is fun to watch everyone try to fly over the brook and to see just how far you can fly.

EXCHANGE

NUMBER OF KIDS: 7 or more

AGES: any (better for younger kids)

TIME ALLOTTED: 15 minutes or more

PLAYING FIELD: any small, open area

EQUIPMENT: none

START-UP: Players choose "It" and everyone else gathers around the It in a circle.

OBJECT: To avoid being It.

PLAY: The It calls out the names of two players in the circle. These players then attempt to switch places. At the same time, the It tries to jump into one of their places in the circle. The It must start in the middle of the circle and no one can move until both names are called. Whoever does not get one of the two open spots is the It for the next round. Play continues until players decide to stop.

An option is that everyone can make up funny names and those can be used.

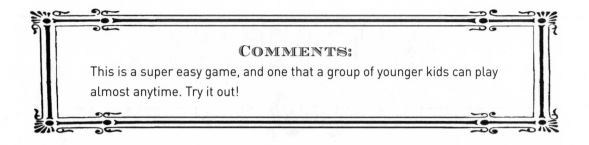

COMMENTS:

This is a super easy game, and one that a group of younger kids can play almost anytime. Try it out!

FOUR SQUARE

NUMBER OF KIDS: 4 or more

AGES: any

TIME ALLOTTED: at least 30 minutes

PLAYING FIELD: a driveway or paved area with large squares or where squares can be drawn with chalk

EQUIPMENT: 1 playground ball or basketball and chalk if necessary to draw squares

START-UP: Players should choose a ball and find a driveway that is divided into squares or draw large squares on the pavement in a safe location. Each player is assigned a square. If there are too many players, the others form a line outside the squares and rotate into play. Designate squares as *A*, *B*, *C*, *D*, and perhaps *E* and *F* if there are enough players and six squares are desired.

OBJECT: To be in the *A* square.

PLAY: Everyone gets into their assigned squares. The person in the *A* square begins with the ball and gets to make the rules at the beginning of each point. That player then serves the ball to another square. If the ball lands in a player's square, that player must hit the ball into another square safely and within the rules established by the person in the *A* square. A player must hit or catch the ball (depending on the current set of rules) before it lands or after one bounce, but the player cannot leave his or her square to do so (unless going for a save—which is when the ball has landed in one's square and bounced past the player and he or she has no choice but to leave his or her square to chase the ball). A point continues until one person gets out. If the player does not touch the ball or does so in a manner not permitted by the current set of rules, he or she is out. If at any time, the ball bounces twice before a player can get to it, that player is out. If a player breaks the rules (designated by the server in *A*) while handling it at any time, that player is out. If a player hits the ball out of bounds or into his or her own square, that player is out.

If for any of these reasons a player gets out, he or she must go to the last square or to the back of the line. Everyone then moves up one square accordingly (for example, if the player in *B* gets out, the player in *C* moves to *B*, the player in *D* moves to *C*, and so on). As long as the same person is in *A*, the rules do not change unless the person in the *A* square specifically announces new rules. As soon as a new person takes the *A* square, that player makes his or her own rules. Play continues until the players are ready to stop.

If no special rules are desired by the *A* square, "clean" play constitutes only bumping the ball into another square. This rule means no catching, clean serves, only one bounce, no hitting the balls into the corners, no spikes, and so on. This can be called by saying "clean."

The rules for each round are generally chosen from the following list of options. The person in the *A* square picks as many as he or she would like or can create his or her own:

CATCHING: one is allowed to catch the ball, carry it, and throw it.

BOBBLES: instead of catching the ball, one is allowed to bobble it temporarily by knocking it between their hands or up into the air without letting it bounce.

SHOE SHINERS: one may never peg another person, but this rule allows the ball to be thrown against another player's shoe to get him or her out.

SKYSCRAPERS: this is when the ball is slammed down in another's square, so that it bounces high and far to get someone out.

TINY TIM: this is when the ball is barely dropped or tapped into another square so it hardly bounces at all.

CORNERS: this allows one to hit dirty shots into the corners of another's square.

FAST THROW: this allows for hard hits or fast throws (only effective when catching is allowed).

SPINS: one can put crazy spins on the ball to make it harder for another to catch (only truly effective when catching is allowed).

DIRTY SERVES: allows the *A* player to serve the ball using any of these types of plays. Dirty serves should not be used as a rule very often.

AROUND THE WORLD: Each player must hit the ball into the square immediately lower than his or her own (*A* to *B*, *B* to *C*, and so on). If the ball gets to the lowest square, he or she must hit it back to the *A* square, and so forth.

DOUBLES: for one turn, pairs (such as *A* with *B* and *C* with *D*) can be made to play as teams. Both players in a pair become out if one of the members makes an error.

CREATE A RULE: use only left hands, and so on.

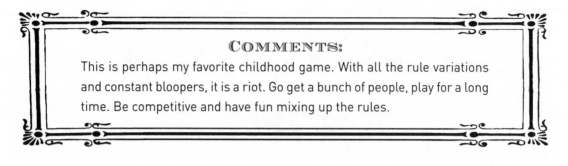

This is perhaps my favorite childhood game. With all the rule variations and constant bloopers, it is a riot. Go get a bunch of people, play for a long time. Be competitive and have fun mixing up the rules.

Variant:

PADDLE FOUR SQUARE: This game uses the same rules with paddles. In this version, be careful that players are far enough apart that they do not risk hitting one another!

Variant:

TWO SQUARE: All the same rules can apply with simply two people. In this game, players should take turns serving and should play to a certain number of points, such as ten.

GARAGE BALL TAG

NUMBER OF KIDS: at least 3

AGES: any

TIME ALLOTTED: 15 minutes or more

PLAYING FIELD: a garage or an open wall

EQUIPMENT: 1 ball that is soft and will not hurt players when the ball is thrown

START-UP: Players should select a ball and find a good garage or wall to use. Players also define boundaries against the wall that include side boundaries and a line about twenty feet back from that wall. Then players choose someone to be It.

OBJECT: To avoid being It.

PLAY: Once It is chosen, everyone else gets against the wall and spreads out as desired within the defined boundaries. The It must stand behind the chosen line and attempt to hit other players with the ball. If a throw is missed, It retrieves the ball, again gets behind the line, and tries again. If It is successful in hitting another player with the ball, that player becomes It and play continues. Players may run and dodge the ball in any way they choose, as long as they stay against the wall. Players may also catch the ball to avoid becoming It. If the ball is caught, it is tossed back to It and play continues. The game continues until the players want to stop.

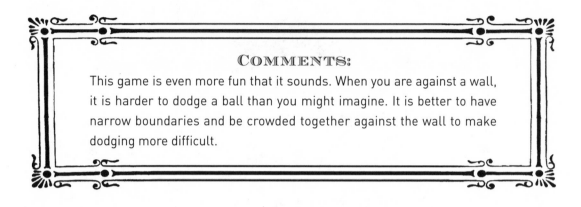

COMMENTS:

This game is even more fun that it sounds. When you are against a wall, it is harder to dodge a ball than you might imagine. It is better to have narrow boundaries and be crowded together against the wall to make dodging more difficult.

HAND SLAP

NUMBER OF KIDS: 2 or more

AGES: 8 and up

TIME ALLOTTED: 15 minutes or more

PLAYING FIELD: a small, open area

EQUIPMENT: one 2 × 4 board or a long, flat log

START-UP: Players should set the 2 × 4 or log on the ground and stand on top of it facing each other, with their feet parallel to the log with one foot in front of the other.

OBJECT: To knock the other player off the board.

PLAY: While on the board, players extend their hands and touch palms. As soon as the palms touch, the game begins. The players then try to knock each other off by slapping or pushing on the other player's hands without grabbing until one loses his or her balance and falls off the board or log. Players must keep both palms facing the other player. No part of the body can be struck except the hand. The last one standing on the board is the winner. If both players fall off at the same time, it is a draw.

COMMENTS:

This game is good for quick competition and balance practice. It's fun to watch and play, but be careful only to slap palms and not to hurt the other player in any way. Mix up your strategy and enjoy the action!

HIDE-AND-SEEK

NUMBER OF KIDS: at least 4

AGES: any

TIME ALLOTTED: 45 minutes or more

PLAYING FIELD: several connecting neighborhood yards (front and back) or a large area with places to hide, such as a park

EQUIPMENT: none

START-UP: Players should define boundaries and choose someone to be It.

OBJECT: To avoid being It.

PLAY: The It begins by counting to sixty while everyone else runs and hides. After counting to sixty, the It announces, "Ready or not, here I come!" The It then begins to search for everyone who is hiding. The first person found is It in the next round. When a player is found, call everyone else to come out of hiding and play again.

Another variation can be the It searches until he or she finds everyone. Then the last person found chooses the next It (but cannot choose the person who is currently It).

Another variation can be that once a person is found, he or she joins the It and helps search for others until only one person is left. The last person found chooses the next It (but cannot choose the person who is currently It).

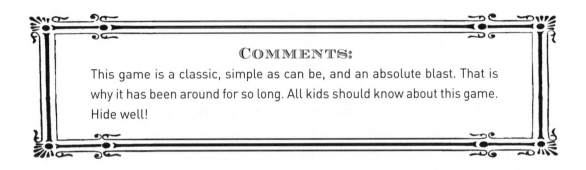

COMMENTS:

This game is a classic, simple as can be, and an absolute blast. That is why it has been around for so long. All kids should know about this game. Hide well!

HOPSCOTCH

NUMBER OF KIDS: at least 2

AGES: any

TIME ALLOTTED: 20 minutes or more

PLAYING FIELD: any safe pavement or sidewalk where chalk drawings can be made

EQUIPMENT: 1 rock for each player and 1 piece of chalk

START-UP: Players should draw a series of boxes on the pavement using a piece of chalk. These boxes need to be connected and can be one or two boxes wide. They should also be numbered, counting up from one, with box 1 being the closest to the starting line. After the boxes are drawn, players choose a throwing order. They should then determine how many rounds will be played or how many points one must get to win.

OBJECT: To score the most points or to finish first.

PLAY: The first player tosses his or her rock into the series of boxes. Observe the number of the box where the rock landed. This is the number of points the player will get for a successful run. A successful run is made by hopping to the rock, picking it up, and getting back across the starting line without messing up. The trick is that each box along the way can only be stepped in once. For a single box, players must hop using only one foot. If the boxes are two wide, players may hop landing on two feet (one in each box) or each box must be hopped in sequentially with one foot (for more advanced players). If a player can follow the hopping pattern, bend over, pick up the rock, and hop back to the start (in the same fashion) without messing up or falling down, that player earns the number of points in the box where his or her rock fell. The winner is the first to the selected number of points or whoever has the highest point total after a chosen number of rounds.

Another version of play can be used where each player must make a successful run in each box, starting with 1 and ending with the highest number. The first player must make a successful run after landing his or her rock in box 1, then box 2, and so on. A player continues until he or she makes a mistake in hopping or throws the rock into the wrong box. The next round that player continues in the box where he or she made the mistake in the previous round. The first person who is successful in completing each box is the winner.

COMMENTS:

This is a classic game that is good for younger kids. If you have never tried this game, give it a shot.

INDIAN WRESTLING

NUMBER OF KIDS: 2, but can be done with more

AGES: any

TIME ALLOTTED: 10 minutes or more

PLAYING FIELD: any area with semisoft ground, such as grass

EQUIPMENT: none

START-UP: Whoever wishes to wrestle lines up within the selected area. Players line up by sitting down hip to hip, facing opposite directions. Players then lay back so they are still lying in opposite directions (so a player's head is roughly next to the other players' heel). The players' hips should still be touching.

OBJECT: To push the opponent over into a backward somersault.

PLAY: Once lined up, a start similar to a face-off occurs. Each player's inside leg is raised so that the opponents' feet touch. They then lower their legs back to the ground. This is done twice. At the third leg raise, both opponents pull their inside leg back a little further so they can hook each other's legs between the foot and knee. The wrestlers then use leverage to try to lower their leg, forcing the opponent's body to roll over backward. The winner, of course, is the one who pushes over the other.

A variant is that the wrestlers should stand up and line up one foot toe-to-toe (right foot to right foot, or left foot to left foot) and grab wrists (of the same side of the body as the aligned foot). Players should put the other leg behind them for support. The wrestlers then count to three and say, "Go!" The goal is to try to pull the opponent across the middle—the point where their toes are touching. The winner is the wrestler who successfully pulls the opponent over the middle.

COMMENTS:
This is an easy but fun game to brag about, and it's enjoyable to watch! They are quite different than most other competitions. It is a great time coming up with unique strategies. Grab an opponent and see how you do!

LOG ROLL

NUMBER OF KIDS: at least 2

AGES: any

TIME ALLOTTED: 10 minutes or more

PLAYING FIELD: any open, grassy area

EQUIPMENT: 1 log

START-UP: Players should find a good, round log and an open area to set it. Each player then steps on top of the log.

OBJECT: To be the last player on the log.

PLAY: One player yells, "Ready, set, go!" and the game begins. Players then try to shake the other players off the log by rocking the log back and forth. Physical contact is not allowed, but anything else goes. If a player touches the ground in any way, the player is eliminated and must walk away from the log. Play continues until only one player is left on the log. That player is the winner.

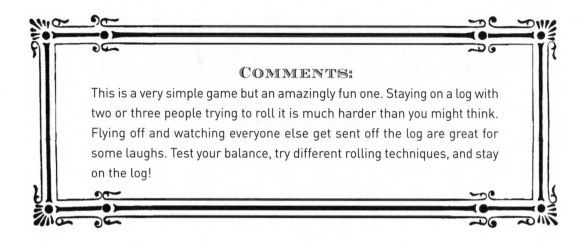

COMMENTS:

This is a very simple game but an amazingly fun one. Staying on a log with two or three people trying to roll it is much harder than you might think. Flying off and watching everyone else get sent off the log are great for some laughs. Test your balance, try different rolling techniques, and stay on the log!

MONKEY IN THE MIDDLE

NUMBER OF KIDS: 3 or more

AGES: any

TIME ALLOTTED: 10 minutes or more

PLAYING FIELD: a yard or open grassy area

EQUIPMENT: 1 ball or other tossable object

START-UP: Players should set boundaries and choose the monkey (or monkeys, if there are enough people) to be in the middle. There is one object tossed per monkey in the middle.

OBJECT: To avoid being the monkey.

PLAY: Everyone circles around the monkey and tosses the object back and forth. The monkey tries to steal the object from the other players while it is in the air or on the ground. The monkey cannot take the object out of someone else's hands, but he or she may do anything else (without touching other players) to get the object. If the monkey does gain possession of the object, the person responsible takes the monkey's place and the game continues. The game ends when players feel like stopping.

COMMENTS:

This game is also referred to as Keep-Away and is one that everyone may already know, but it is a classic, easy to play, and fun.

PALM BOXING

NUMBER OF KIDS: 2 (more than 2 can take turns)

AGES: 8 and up

TIME ALLOTTED: 10 minutes or more

PLAYING FIELD: a small, open area

EQUIPMENT: none

START-UP: The two players stand close together. They face each other and push their own heels together.

OBJECT: To knock the other player off balance causing them to move one or both feet.

PLAY: When in position, the opponents reach out and put their palms together. As soon as their palms touch, the round begins. Keeping their palms against their opponent's palms, the boxers try to push each other off balance by pushing with one or both hands. Players can move their bodies around, leaning side to side, and so on, but they may not move their feet. The first player to move one or both feet loses the contest.

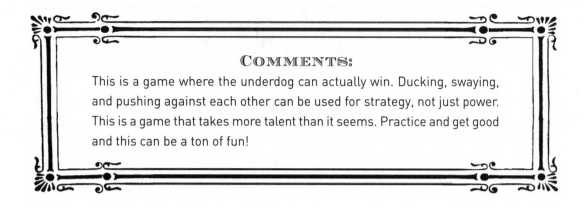

COMMENTS:

This is a game where the underdog can actually win. Ducking, swaying, and pushing against each other can be used for strategy, not just power. This is a game that takes more talent than it seems. Practice and get good and this can be a ton of fun!

POISON CIRCLE

NUMBER OF KIDS: 2 teams of at least 2

AGES: 8 and up

TIME ALLOTTED: 25 minutes or more

PLAYING FIELD: an open, grassy area

EQUIPMENT: anything to mark a circle, for example, string or rope. If these are not available, the game can be played with a square that can be marked using cones or any objects to mark the corners.

START-UP: Teams are chosen and a circle is drawn or marked on the grass. Both teams should spread out around the outside of the circle. Each player should have an opponent on each side. Everyone joins hands.

OBJECT: To be the surviving player.

PLAY: The game begins as one player yells, "Ready, set, go!" Everyone then tries to pull their opponents into the circle without stepping into the circle themselves. As soon as one person steps in the circle, play instantly stops (so that only one player is eliminated at a time). The player who stepped in the circle first is eliminated. Hands are held once again to form a new circle, and a new round ensues. Shrink the circle as necessary as players are eliminated. The team with the last remaining player(s) is the winner.

COMMENTS:

This is a fantastic version of tug-of-war. It's fun and chaotic. It may get messy, but it is fun to watch everyone pull and fall. Try leaning back and pulling forward. Finding the right balance is tougher than it sounds. Play hard and don't be afraid to get a little physical with this game.

PRISONERS' ATTACK

NUMBER OF KIDS: 2 teams of at least 3

AGES: any

TIME ALLOTTED: 30 minutes or more

PLAYING FIELD: any large, open, grassy area or field

EQUIPMENT: 1 ball

START-UP: Players should define boundaries that include two even-sized rectangular or circular playing areas with a large neutral area in between them. Boundaries also include a prison area behind each playing area. Players should then choose teams and each team goes to its playing area.

OBJECT: To imprison all of the opponents.

PLAY: One player starts with the ball. That player's team can pass it among themselves or throw it toward the other team's playing area. When a player throws the ball toward the other playing area, he or she must call out an opponent's name at the same time that the ball is thrown. Someone on the other team must then catch the ball before it lands within his or her playing area. If a catch is not made and the ball lands in the playing area, the player whose name was called must go to the other team's prison. The other team then throws the ball back in the same fashion. If the ball lands in neutral territory or anywhere out of bounds, the throw is wasted and the other team gets the ball. Teams throw the ball back and forth until all the players on one team are imprisoned.

Players get out of prison if a bad throw lands in their prison area. The player can then pick up the ball and try to hit a player on the other team with the ball. The ball must hit the other player in the air without being caught by anyone on the opposing team. If successful, the prisoner returns to his or her playing area.

Play always stops when a player is entering or leaving jail, and the ball switches possession after each throw. If a prisoner attempts to free him- or herself (successfully or unsuccessfully), the ball goes to the other team (not the prisoner's team) afterward. Once a team has imprisoned everyone on the other team, the game is over and that team wins.

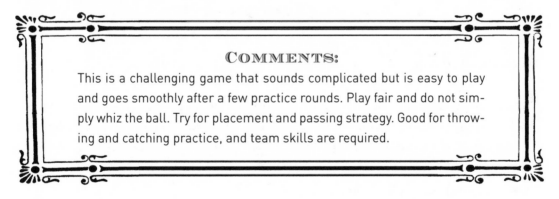

COMMENTS:

This is a challenging game that sounds complicated but is easy to play and goes smoothly after a few practice rounds. Play fair and do not simply whiz the ball. Try for placement and passing strategy. Good for throwing and catching practice, and team skills are required.

VARIANT: Play every player for him- or herself. Each player gets a little playing area of his or her own and is eliminated from play instead of going to prison. The players' areas should be equally spread with some neutral area in between. The player that tosses the ball still calls out the person's name. Players are eliminated if their toss lands outside of the playing area of the player he or she called or if the player drops the balls when his or her name is called. If a player eliminates someone, he or she gets the ball back.

RED ROVER

NUMBER OF KIDS: 2 teams of at least 4

AGES: any

TIME ALLOTTED: 30 minutes or more

PLAYING FIELD: a large yard or grassy area

EQUIPMENT: none

START-UP: Players choose two teams. Each team gets in a side-by-side line, one team facing the other, about ten yards apart. Each player grabs the wrist or hand of each person next to him or her.

OBJECT: To capture each opponent.

PLAY: One team is chosen to go first. The team confers and decides on a player from the other team to challenge. Everyone on the challenging team says, "Red rover, red rover, send (player's name) over." The player called then leaves his or her line and charges toward the challenging team's line. The challenged player must try to break through the opponent's line by charging *between* (not over) two players, breaking their arms apart. If he or she cannot break the chain, that player is captured and must join the chain where he or she failed to break it. If the challenged player successfully breaks the chain, that player gets to return to his or her original line and to bring back one of the two players where the chain broke. Then the other team calls a player and the process repeats. The teams go back and forth until one team is the clear winner, usually when only one or two players are left on a side. One option can be that when one player is left, he or she has one last chance to break the opponent's chain, or the game is over. Once the game is over, form new teams and play again.

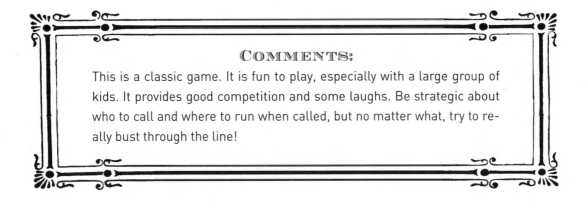

COMMENTS:

This is a classic game. It is fun to play, especially with a large group of kids. It provides good competition and some laughs. Be strategic about who to call and where to run when called, but no matter what, try to really bust through the line!

TREASURE HUNT

NUMBER OF KIDS: 2 or more

AGES: any

TIME ALLOTTED: 45 minutes or more

PLAYING FIELD: a large safe area, such as several connecting yards or a park

EQUIPMENT: 1 or more treasures to find and materials to make clues, such as paper and pencil

START-UP: One child or adult organizes the hunt, which includes making and hiding a series of clues for the other players to follow and hiding the final treasure(s).

OBJECT: To successfully decipher the clues to find the treasure.

PLAY: After the organizer has made and hidden all the clues and the treasure, the other players are called to begin. They are given the first clue at the designated starting point and the hunt begins. Of course, the game ends when the players successfully solve all the clues and end up finding the treasure. Take turns creating the hunts.

One option, instead of writing clues, is that one player simply hides a series of objects in a given area and the winner is the player who finds the most objects.

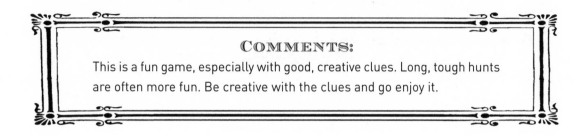

TUG-OF-WAR

NUMBER OF KIDS: 2 teams of at least 2

AGES: any

TIME ALLOTTED: 10 minutes or more

PLAYING FIELD: any open strip of ground

EQUIPMENT: 1 long, thick rope

START-UP: Players define a middle line and choose teams. Teams separate, with one team on each side of the middle line. Make sure exactly half of the rope lies on each side of the middle line. Everyone picks up the rope and braces themselves.

OBJECT: To pull the front person of the other team over the middle line.

PLAY: Once everyone has a good hold of the rope, one player says, "Ready, set, pull!" and both teams begin to pull. Play continues until one of the players closest to the middle line is pulled over the line. The team who pulls the other player over the middle line is the winner.

COMMENTS:

This is a fun and easy game. It's a classic, and a must play!

 # ACTIVITY LEVEL III

1, 2, 3 ... I SPY

NUMBER OF KIDS: at least 4

AGES: any

TIME ALLOTTED: at least 45 minutes

PLAYING FIELD: several connecting neighborhood yards (front and back) or a large area with places to hide, such as a park

EQUIPMENT: none

START-UP: Players define boundaries, choose a base (such as a porch or fence), and select someone to be It.

OBJECT: To avoid being It.

PLAY: The It guards the base and closes his or her eyes and counts to a number, usually fifty, to give the other players a chance to disperse and hide. The It then tries to do two things: to find the other players and to protect the base. The other players also have two goals: to not be spotted and to reach base before being called.

If the It sees someone at any time, he or she "calls" that player by returning to base, maintaining contact with it, and yelling loudly, "One, two, three, I spy (the player's name and hiding location)." For example, the It could yell, "One, two, three, I spy Jane behind the red car." If the It is correct in naming the player and his or her location, the game is over. The called player is It for the next round and the game restarts. If the It is wrong, play resumes (guessing is not allowed!).

While the It is trying to find people, the other players wait for a chance to break toward base. The players do not have to stay in one hiding place, but can move around within the given boundaries. If a player breaks towards base and can touch it and yell "safe" before being called, that player is safe and watches until the next round. The It may call a player running toward base by saying, "One, two, three, I spy (player's name) running in." The It must complete the whole phrase loudly before that person contacts the base and yells "safe."

When a player is called successfully by the It, everyone still hiding returns to base and the new round begins. If everyone reaches base safely, the last player that arrived is It for the next round..

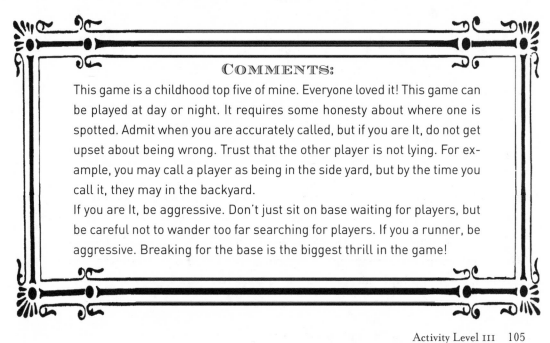

COMMENTS:

This game is a childhood top five of mine. Everyone loved it! This game can be played at day or night. It requires some honesty about where one is spotted. Admit when you are accurately called, but if you are It, do not get upset about being wrong. Trust that the other player is not lying. For example, you may call a player as being in the side yard, but by the time you call it, they may in the backyard.

If you are It, be aggressive. Don't just sit on base waiting for players, but be careful not to wander too far searching for players. If you a runner, be aggressive. Breaking for the base is the biggest thrill in the game!

ARMY

Number of kids: at least 2

Ages: any

Time allotted: 15 minutes or more

Playing field: any large area with obstacles and places to hide

---

Equipment: players' choice of anything that could be used in a pretend battle (plastic guns, water guns, cap guns, even sticks that can be pretend guns)

Start-up: Players define boundaries and split up into two teams.

Object: To win the fake battle.

Play: There are not too many rules to this game. Players simply spread out within boundaries and the battle begins. Players try to sneak up on each other and yell, "Bang!" with their weapons pointed at an opponent. If an opponent is "hit," he or she lies down and plays dead until the battle has ended. The winner is the team who has the last remaining players.

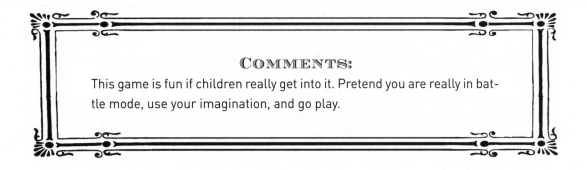

COMMENTS:

This game is fun if children really get into it. Pretend you are really in battle mode, use your imagination, and go play.

BALL PUNCH

NUMBER OF KIDS: at least 5

AGES: any

TIME ALLOTTED: 15 minutes or more

PLAYING FIELD: any small, open area

EQUIPMENT: 1 large ball (such as a playground ball)

START-UP: One player is chosen to be It and everyone else stands in a circle. The It begins outside the circle of players.

OBJECT: To avoid being It.

PLAY: One player begins with the ball and passes it to the player on his or her left. Players then continue to pass the ball to the left. While this is occurring, the It is trying to punch the ball while it is being passed. The It cannot hit the ball out of anyone's hands, but can hit it anytime it is in the air or on the ground. The It must remain outside the circle at all times. If the It successfully interrupts a pass by hitting the ball, the player who allowed the hit to occur becomes It and changes places with the former It.

COMMENTS:

The size of the circle makes a big difference in this game. Try changing the distance between players to find the best game. Overall, this is a fun, fast-paced game that's definitely worth a try.

BREAK AND RUN

NUMBER OF KIDS: at least 7

AGES: 8 and up

TIME ALLOTTED: 30 minutes or more

PLAYING FIELD: any large, open area

EQUIPMENT: none

START-UP: Players pick one person to be the bull and another to be the keeper. Everyone else forms a ring of people by joining hands or wrists. The bull gets into the middle of the ring, and the keeper is on the outside.

OBJECT: To get the bull out of the ring (for the bull and keeper), and to keep the bull inside the ring, then tag the bull and keeper when the bull escapes (for everyone else).

PLAY: The keeper counts to three, says "Go!" and the game begins. The bull and the keeper then do whatever they can (without using violence) to get the bull out of the ring. Pushing, pulling, and maneuvering are all allowed, but being overly physical is not. The bull and the keeper cannot team up against one player in the ring. The keeper also cannot enter the ring. Players forming the ring move or block the bull, but players cannot "break the ring" by releasing each other's hands or wrists. Once the bull breaks loose or the ring is broken, the bull and the keeper should run off as fast as possible. All the other players in the ring break apart and try to tag the keeper and bull. Whoever tags them takes their place in the next round. Because everyone will want to be the bull, if a player has already been bull once, he or she should choose another player who has not had a turn yet.

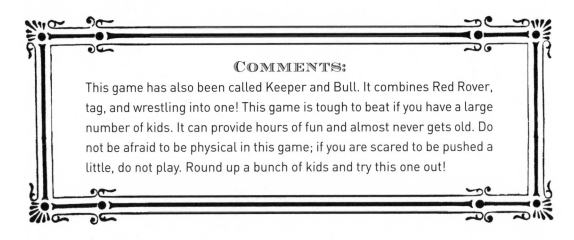

COMMENTS:

This game has also been called Keeper and Bull. It combines Red Rover, tag, and wrestling into one! This game is tough to beat if you have a large number of kids. It can provide hours of fun and almost never gets old. Do not be afraid to be physical in this game; if you are scared to be pushed a little, do not play. Round up a bunch of kids and try this one out!

CIRCLE CHASE

NUMBER OF KIDS: at least 8

AGES: any

TIME ALLOTTED: 25 minutes or more

PLAYING FIELD: a yard or large grassy area

EQUIPMENT: none

START-UP: Players choose a chaser and a runner. Everyone else gets into a circle, with the runner on the inside and the chaser on the outside.

OBJECT: For the chaser to catch the runner.

PLAY: Everyone in the circle joins hands. The runner says, "Go!" and the game begins. The chaser then tries to break into the circle to catch the runner. The players in the circle try to keep the chaser out (without getting rough). The runner can leave the circle to escape, but if he or she does, everyone in the circle drops hands. When the runner reenters, the players in the circle rejoin hands. This goes on until the chaser catches the runner. The runner and chaser then choose their replacements and another round ensues. Players can play as many rounds as desired.

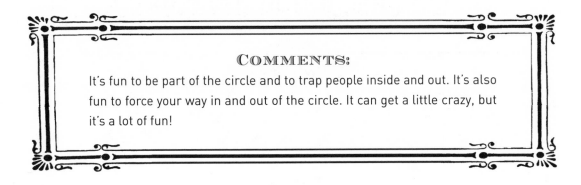

COMMENTS:

It's fun to be part of the circle and to trap people inside and out. It's also fun to force your way in and out of the circle. It can get a little crazy, but it's a lot of fun!

COPS AND ROBBERS

NUMBER OF KIDS: 2 teams of at least 2

AGES: any

TIME ALLOTTED: 20 minutes or more

PLAYING FIELD: a yard or large grassy area

EQUIPMENT: none

START-UP: Players should define a field of play with two end lines and choose two even teams of cops and robbers. The cops all line up on the end line of the field and close their eyes. The robbers begin at the opposite end line on the field.

OBJECT: The cops try to capture all the robbers.

PLAY: Play begins when the cops turn around and close their eyes and the robbers begin to move toward the cops. The robbers try to get as close to the cops as possible without being heard. The cops, keeping their eyes closed, try to hear the robbers get closer. At any time, a cop can call out, "robbers!" When that is called out, all the cops can open their eyes. The cops then try to tag the robbers.

The robbers must then run back to their end line on the field before being tagged. If a robber is tagged, he or she is out of the game. If, however, a robber makes it all the way across the field to the cops' end line before "Robber!" is called, he or she cannot be tagged in that round. The rounds continue until one robber is left. That robber is the winner. The cops and robbers then switch teams and a new round is played.

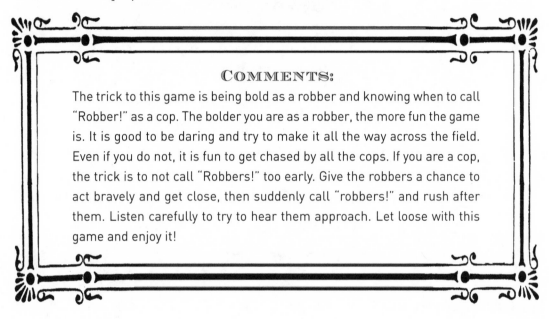

COMMENTS:

The trick to this game is being bold as a robber and knowing when to call "Robber!" as a cop. The bolder you are as a robber, the more fun the game is. It is good to be daring and try to make it all the way across the field. Even if you do not, it is fun to get chased by all the cops. If you are a cop, the trick is to not call "Robbers!" too early. Give the robbers a chance to act bravely and get close, then suddenly call "robbers!" and rush after them. Listen carefully to try to hear them approach. Let loose with this game and enjoy it!

GHOST IN THE GRAVEYARD

NUMBER OF KIDS: at least 3

AGES: any

TIME ALLOTTED: at least 45 minutes

PLAYING FIELD: several connecting neighborhood yards (front and back) or a large area with places to hide, such as a park

EQUIPMENT: none

START-UP: Players define boundaries, "the graveyard," choose a base (such as a fence or lamppost), and select a "ghost."

OBJECT: For the ghost to catch players before they reach base.

PLAY: The game begins when everyone but the ghost closes their eyes to count while the ghost runs to hide. The group can count to fifty, but traditionally the group counts together as follows:

"One o'clock, two o'clock, three o'clock o'rock.
Four o'clock, five o'clock, six o'clock o'rock.
Seven o'clock, eight o'clock, nine o'clock, o'rock.
Ten o'clock, eleven o'clock, twelve o'clock, o'rock midnight (yelled)!"

Then the players spread out and search for the "ghost in the graveyard." If a player spots the ghost or if the ghost jumps out, the player who sees him or her first instantly yells, "Ghost in the graveyard!" Once this is called, everyone tries to reach base before being tagged by the ghost. If a player touches the base, he or she is safe from being tagged. The first player the ghost tags is the ghost for the next round. If everyone makes it to base safely, the same ghost hides again. Play continues as long as players want.

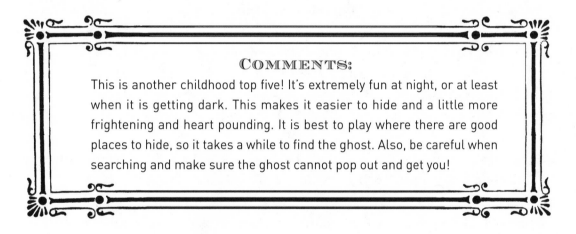

COMMENTS:

This is another childhood top five! It's extremely fun at night, or at least when it is getting dark. This makes it easier to hide and a little more frightening and heart pounding. It is best to play where there are good places to hide, so it takes a while to find the ghost. Also, be careful when searching and make sure the ghost cannot pop out and get you!

KICK THE CAN

NUMBER OF KIDS: 2 teams of at least 2

AGES: any

TIME ALLOTTED: at least 45 minutes

PLAYING FIELD: several connecting neighborhood yards (front and back) or a large area with places to hide, such as a park

EQUIPMENT: 1 can. Tins cans are best because they will not blow over with the wind, but a soda can, empty bucket, etc., can be substituted if necessary.

START-UP: Players should set boundaries, choose two teams, and set the can in a safe place in the center of the boundaries. One team is designated as the kickers (offense) and the other as the chasers (defense). Players can alter how many kickers and chasers there are to vary the difficulty of being on offense or defense.

OBJECT: The chasers try to tag all the kickers and the kickers try to kick the can.

PLAY: The chasers huddle around the can, close their eyes, and count to a number (usually fifty) to give the kickers a chance to disperse and hide. The chasers then try to do two things: to find and tag the kickers and to protect the can. If a chaser manages to tag a kicker, that kicker is out for the round and must wait on the side until the round ends. The chasers win if all the kickers are successfully caught before the can is kicked. If a kicker manages to reach the can and kick it without being tagged, the game is over. The kickers win. After a winner is found, everyone is called to return to the middle. Switch teams and begin a new round. One round at a time can be played, or the teams can play a series, in which a point is earned for every time the can is successfully kicked.

COMMENTS:

This is perhaps *the* classic game! It is extremely fun even though it is so simple! If you have never played this, get out there and try it. There is a reason it is such a classic: it is easy to play and makes for hours of fun!

MANHUNT

NUMBER OF KIDS: at least 5

AGES: 8 and up

TIME ALLOTTED: 1 hour or more

PLAYING FIELD: a large area with hiding places and space to roam, such as an entire block of yards, a large forest area, a park, or a large playground

EQUIPMENT: none

START-UP: Players define large boundaries, usually a neighborhood block. Players then choose a base and pick teams. One team is chosen to be the hunters and the others are the prisoners. Usually one to three extra players are chosen to be hunters so there are more hunters than prisoners.

OBJECT: For the hunters to find and bring to base all the prisoners.

PLAY: The hunters remain on base for three minutes while the prisoners run and hide anywhere within the boundaries. The hunters then split up and begin to look for the prisoners. Prisoners may stay on the move or hide. If spotted, a prisoner can run. To capture a prisoner, the hunter must wrap both arms around the prisoner. The prisoner must then accept capture and go with the hunter back to base. The base then becomes the prison for the captured prisoner. Jailbreaks are possible in this game, but only one prisoner can be freed at a time. To free a prisoner, another prisoner player who has not been captured yet must touch hands with a captured prisoner. They both must then run off and can be captured at any time during this process. Because prisoners are difficult to catch, the prisoners cannot return right away to attempt to free more prisoners; they must wait at least a few minutes. The game ends when all the prisoners have been successfully caught or when the hunters give up.

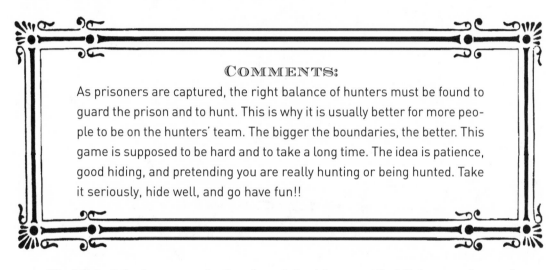

COMMENTS:

As prisoners are captured, the right balance of hunters must be found to guard the prison and to hunt. This is why it is usually better for more people to be on the hunters' team. The bigger the boundaries, the better. This game is supposed to be hard and to take a long time. The idea is patience, good hiding, and pretending you are really hunting or being hunted. Take it seriously, hide well, and go have fun!!

Flashlight Manhunt can also be played. In this game, flashlights may be used at night to capture prisoners instead of wrapping arms around them.

Another option is to simply tag prisoners in order to capture them, especially for younger children.

Variant:

RINGALEVIO: This is a similar game but is played in a smaller area (maybe two yards, front and back). The jail should be a larger circle in the middle of the playing field. To capture a prisoner, a hunter only needs to tag him or her. To free a prisoner, an uncaptured prisoner must enter the jail circle and yell the player's name and "Ringalevio." The game ends when all the prisoners are caught.

MAYPOLE

NUMBER OF KIDS: at least 3

AGES: any

TIME ALLOTTED: 20 minutes or more

PLAYING FIELD: a pole or an open tree trunk

EQUIPMENT: 1 long strip of ribbon of equal length for each player

START-UP: Each player gets a piece of ribbon and ties one end of it to the top of the pole. Players then walk away from the pole, holding the other end of the ribbon so it stretches to full length. Players spread out evenly around the pole.

OBJECT: To decorate the pole.

PLAY: One player yells "Go!" and the game begins. Half of the players should begin running clockwise and the other half should run counterclockwise around the pole. The players weave inside and outside of each other in a random fashion. This will leave a great pattern of woven ribbons on the pole that all players can enjoy. The ribbon should be taken down when players are finished and multiple rounds can be played. Each round will leave a unique pattern!

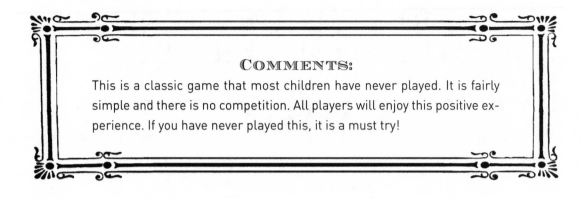

COMMENTS:

This is a classic game that most children have never played. It is fairly simple and there is no competition. All players will enjoy this positive experience. If you have never played this, it is a must try!

ONE MAN TOSS UP

NUMBER OF KIDS: at least 4

AGES: any

TIME ALLOTTED: at least 30 minutes

PLAYING FIELD: a large, open yard or field

EQUIPMENT: 1 ball that is soft and will not hurt players when thrown

START-UP: Players should choose a ball, define roughly circular boundaries, and pick one player to be the first tosser.

OBJECT: To avoid being the tosser.

PLAY: Everyone gathers near the tosser as he or she throws the ball into the air. The tosser then calls out a name and everyone scatters. The tosser tries to run into a safe area away from other players but must stay in bounds. The person whose name was called must get the ball and yell "Stop!" At this, everyone but the tosser must stop moving. The ball is then allowed to be passed three times, but it can never touch the ground. The object is to try to hit the tosser (who is allowed to run and dodge) using three passes or fewer and a throw. If someone hits the tosser (before the ball hits the ground), then the tosser is It again. If not, the person who threw and missed the tosser or let the ball hit the ground is the tosser for the next round. Play ends when all players agree to stop.

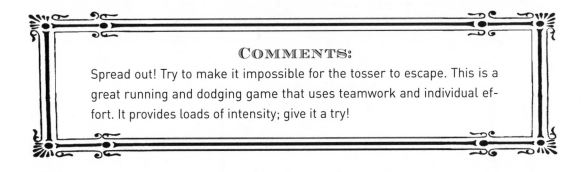

COMMENTS:

Spread out! Try to make it impossible for the tosser to escape. This is a great running and dodging game that uses teamwork and individual effort. It provides loads of intensity; give it a try!

PASS AND OVERTAKE

NUMBER OF KIDS: at least 6

AGES: any

TIME ALLOTTED: 20 minutes or more

PLAYING FIELD: any open area

EQUIPMENT: 1 ball

START-UP: Everyone chooses an order and gets into a single-file line, spaced about four feet apart. The first person in line then takes the ball, chooses a spot about fifteen feet ahead of the next person in line, and stands there.

OBJECT: For the chaser to catch the runner.

PLAY: The first person (who moved up fifteen feet) begins by throwing the ball to the second player in line. Neither player can move until the ball is passed and caught. The person who caught the ball becomes the runner. The runner must then run to the end of the line, weaving in and out of every player in line. The passer tries to catch the runner before he or she completes the trip. If the passer catches the runner, that player earns a point. If the runner escapes, the runner gets the point. When the point is determined, the passer goes to the back of the line and the runner becomes the new passer. A round ends when every player has played both positions once. Play as many rounds as desired. The winner is the player with the most points at the end.

COMMENTS:

Players will have a blast bobbing and weaving in this game. It is exciting, fast paced, and great exercise. Players will have a blast bobbing and weaving in this game. It is exciting, fast paced, and great exercise. Run hard and enjoy it. Play over and over and get a little dizzy!

PEG

Number of kids: at least 2

Ages: 8 and up

Time allotted: at least 15 minutes

Playing field: any driveway or concrete area with a wall at the end (best if the driveway or surface is on a downhill slant)

Equipment: 1 soft bouncy ball (like a tennis ball) and a closed garage or wall

Start-up: Players should form boundaries that include sidelines and a pass line at the end. The pass line should be about ten to fifteen feet down the driveway. The sidelines are usually the sides of the driveway. (If the area is not on a driveway, simply mark makeshift lines with chalk). An order is then chosen and players form a line behind the pass line.

Object: To peg others and to avoid being pegged.

Play: The first person in line takes the ball and throws it against the garage or wall. The next player in line then catches the ball. That player then throws the ball against the wall for the next person. After a player throws the ball, he or she must return to the back of the line.

There are two tricks to this game. The first is that for the throw to be legal, it must cross the designated pass line on the way back, after bouncing off the garage, before it goes out of bounds across a sideline. A player may, of course, catch the ball before it crosses the pass line. The second trick is that the player who attempts to catch the ball must catch it before the ball goes past his or her body in any way.

If the ball is thrown illegally, so that it goes out of bounds, the thrower must run and touch the wall and return across the pass line. During this run, the rest of the players try to grab the ball and peg the runner before he or she returns across the pass line. If a legal throw goes past the catcher's body, the catcher must also make that same run. When the runner passes the pass line after touching the garage, the run is over and that player can no longer be pegged. The player who made the run simply goes to the end of line and whoever is then first in line gets the ball and a new round begins.

There are several ways to end the game. Players can simply play continuously for the thrill of playing. Players can also declare that if someone is hit, that player must sit out until the next round and the winner is the last one standing. Another option is to play so that a point is earned for being hit and a player is out when a certain number of points is reached.

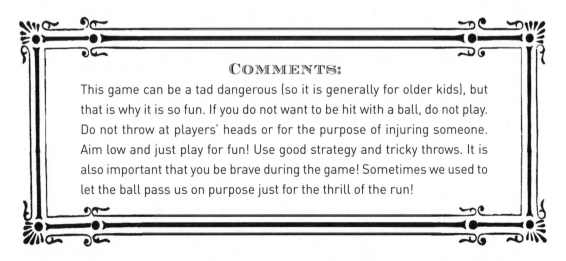

COMMENTS:

This game can be a tad dangerous (so it is generally for older kids), but that is why it is so fun. If you do not want to be hit with a ball, do not play. Do not throw at players' heads or for the purpose of injuring someone. Aim low and just play for fun! Use good strategy and tricky throws. It is also important that you be brave during the game! Sometimes we used to let the ball pass us on purpose just for the thrill of the run!

RED DEVIL

NUMBER OF KIDS: at least 3

AGES: any

TIME ALLOTTED: 20 minutes or more

PLAYING FIELD: a yard with a house or any large object to run around, such as a group of trees, a picnic table, or a swing set

EQUIPMENT: none

START-UP: Players all begin in front of the house (or large object) and choose a player to be the red devil.

OBJECT: To win the races and become the red devil.

PLAY: The first red devil thinks of an object and the category to which it belongs (for example, kiwi and the category "types of fruit"). The red devil then faces the other players and says, "I am thinking of a type of (category name)." The other players then take turns trying to guess what the red devil has thought of. When a correct answer is heard, the red devil announces the name of the player who guessed it correctly. As soon as the name is said, that player and the red devil must run around the house as quickly as possible. The first person back becomes the red devil and a new round begins.

An option is that for tired players or those who do not like to run, a rule can be used that says the first one back is not the red devil. A smaller object to run around can also be chosen, such as a table or tree instead of a house.

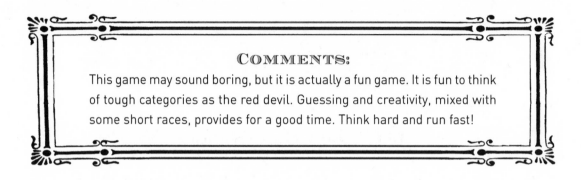

COMMENTS:

This game may sound boring, but it is actually a fun game. It is fun to think of tough categories as the red devil. Guessing and creativity, mixed with some short races, provides for a good time. Think hard and run fast!

SARDINES

NUMBER OF KIDS: at least 4

AGES: any

TIME ALLOTTED: 45 minutes or more

PLAYING FIELD: several connecting neighborhood yards (front and back) or a large area with places to hide, such as a park

EQUIPMENT: none

START-UP: Players should define boundaries and choose someone to be It.

OBJECT: To find the It as soon as possible and to hide with him or her.

PLAY: Play begins as the It runs and hides. Everyone else counts to sixty with their eyes closed. Once sixty is reached, the players scatter to search for the It. If someone finds the It, instead of calling out, that player hides with It. Play continues until everyone has found the original It and has packed into the hiding place like sardines. Then the last player who found the original It is It for the next round. A time limit should be set of about ten or fifteen minutes in case someone cannot find the It's hiding spot. If more than one player is left after the time limit, each remaining player is It for the next round and will hide together. Players can play as many rounds as desired.

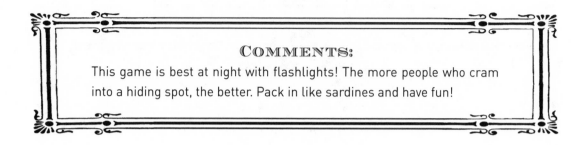

COMMENTS:

This game is best at night with flashlights! The more people who cram into a hiding spot, the better. Pack in like sardines and have fun!

SLAP THE NOSE

NUMBER OF KIDS: at least 4

AGES: any

TIME ALLOTTED: 1 hour or more

PLAYING FIELD: several connecting neighborhood yards (front and back) or a large area with places to hide, such as a park

EQUIPMENT: none

START-UP: Players should define boundaries, pick someone to be It, and choose a base (such as a wall or tree).

OBJECT: To avoid being It.

PLAY: The person who is It hides his or her face against the base. Everyone else gathers behind the It. Someone draws a face on the back of the It using his or her finger. The player describes what he or she is drawing ("Here is the mouth," and so on). Anytime after the nose is drawn, any player, even the drawer, may "slap the nose"—quickly tapping the It on the back where the nose was drawn. The object is to slap the nose so the It does not know who the slapper was. The It must then turn and identify whom he or she thinks the culprit is. The accused slapper says, "How far shall I run and how high shall I count?" The It then pronounces a distance, a direction, and a number. If the It has correctly identified the slapper, the slapper must run the distance and back while counting to the assigned number aloud. If the It was incorrect, then he or she must make the run.

Whoever is punished into running then becomes It for a game of hide-and-seek. While the punished runner is counting and running the assigned distance, everyone else runs and hides. After the distance is run and the number is counted, that person then begins to seek. The first person found is the It who will face the wall. Everyone else is called in and the next round begins. Players can play as many rounds as desired.

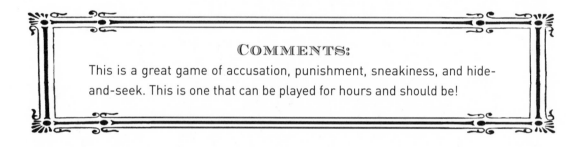

COMMENTS:

This is a great game of accusation, punishment, sneakiness, and hide-and-seek. This is one that can be played for hours and should be!

SPUD

NUMBER OF KIDS: at least 4

AGES: any

TIME ALLOTTED: at least 30 minutes

PLAYING FIELD: a large, open yard or field

EQUIPMENT: 1 playground ball or other soft ball

START-UP: There are no real boundaries, just an open area. Each player counts off a number, starting with one, so that each player has his or her own number.

OBJECT: To not gain the letters *S-P-U-D*.

PLAY: One player starts with the ball and everyone gathers in a circle. The player with the ball throws it straight up into the air and calls out a player's number. All players can begin to spread anywhere as soon as the ball is tossed. Whomever's number is called (and only that player) must catch the ball as soon as possible. When that player catches the ball, he or she yells, "Freeze!" All other players must stop immediately where they are. The player with the ball may then take two large hops in any direction. This player then attempts to hit another player with the ball. The other player must dodge the ball but cannot move until the ball is thrown. If the ball hits the other player before touching the ground, the player who was hit receives the letter *S*. Play continues and the next time the same player is hit, he or she receives the letter *P*, then *U*, and then *D*. If the player with the ball fails to hit someone on the throw attempt, he or she receives a letter. Everyone then comes back together and the player who received a letter gets to toss up the ball and call out the next number, and the entire process repeats. The game ends when one player spells *S-P-U-D*. The winner(s) are the players with the fewest letters.

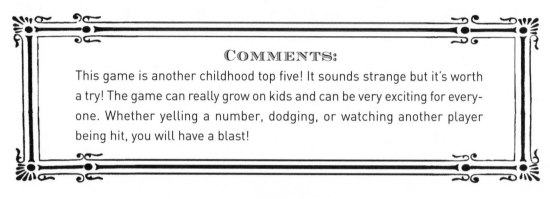

COMMENTS:

This game is another childhood top five! It sounds strange but it's worth a try! The game can really grow on kids and can be very exciting for everyone. Whether yelling a number, dodging, or watching another player being hit, you will have a blast!

Variant:

BUDDY SPUD: This version has teams of two players. When your team's number is called, either player can go for the ball while the teammate runs among the other players. After "Freeze!" is called, everyone must stop, even the teammate of the person who called "Freeze!" The ball is then thrown as described previously, or it can be passed to the teammate. Either player can take the hops, but only two total jumps are allowed. Only one pass is allowed. A pass must also be caught successfully or a letter is earned. Each player of a team earns letters together, not separately. All other rules stand.

Variant:

CALL BALL: In this game, players do not spread out when the ball is thrown. Instead, the game only consists of the initial toss. The player who tosses the ball is It. That player tosses the ball straight up and the player who is called must catch the ball in the air. If the player does not catch it, he or she becomes It, and if the ball is caught, the It remains It and must toss again.

STOOP BALL

NUMBER OF KIDS: at least 2

AGES: any

TIME ALLOTTED: 20 minutes or more

PLAYING FIELD: an open street in front of a building with steps

EQUIPMENT: 1 bouncy ball, such as a racquetball

START-UP: Players split into two teams and define the throwing line. One team begins in the field and the other is up to bat, or the game can be played one-on-one (see options 3 and 4).

OBJECT: To score the most runs.

PLAY: The first player up to bat stands behind the throwing line, faces the building, and throws the ball against the steps as hard as he or she wants. The ball must then strike the steps and ricochet back into the street. The ball must travel in the air at least past the throwing line. Rules similar to baseball then follow. If the ball misses the steps or fails to ricochet past the throwing line, the batter receives a strike. Three strikes and the batter is out. If the ball ricochets past the throwing line, it is in play. This is where several variations have emerged, each of which is explained below.

Options:

1. When a ball is in play, the batter is out if the ball is caught in the air by an opponent. If the ball bounces once before a catch, the batter receives a single (as in baseball). A double is earned if the ball bounces twice, a triple is earned for three bounces, and a home run is earned for four of more bounces. Ghost (pretend) runners should be used in lieu of actual base running. Batters continue to switch and bat until three outs are earned, and then the teams switch. Play any number of innings or up to a certain score.

2. When a ball is in play, the number of bases received is determined strictly by how far the ball travels before it lands. Lines can be marked before the game to indicate a single, double, triple, or home run. Again, the batter is out if three strikes are received or if an opponent catches the ball in the air.

3. For one-on-one play, option 2 can be followed with one rule change. Instead of strikes, outs are received for throws that are not in play.

4. Another one-on-one option is to award a single if the fielder cannot stop the ball cleanly, a double if the ball passes the fielder, and a home run if the ball flies over the fielder's head. For this, a line where the fielder should stand should be marked. Outs are issued if an opponent can catch or cleanly stop the ball before it passes him or her and also for throws that are not in play.

COMMENTS:
This is a classic game that seems to be more popular in big cities but that can be played anywhere. Perfecting the throw is the hardest part of the game, but practicing and playing are nonstop excitement. Find a good area to play and try this out!

SWAT TAG

NUMBER OF KIDS: at least 4

AGES: any

TIME ALLOTTED: 10 minutes or more

PLAYING FIELD: any open area

EQUIPMENT: 1 rolled-up newspaper

START-UP: Players should choose someone to be It. Everyone else gets into a circle and turns to their right with their hands behind their backs. Players must turn so that they are facing the person's back in front of them and must keep their eyes on the back of that player.

OBJECT: To swat the other players as much as possible.

PLAY: The person chosen to be It walks around the outside of the circle and places the newspaper into the hands of one of the other players. This player becomes the swatter and instantly smacks the player in front of him or her below the waist with the newspaper. That person then becomes the runner. The swatter chases the runner around the circle hitting the runner as many times as possible below the waist before the runner returns to his or her original position. The runner then becomes the new It, everyone else gets into a circle again, and the process starts over. Play continues for as long as players want.

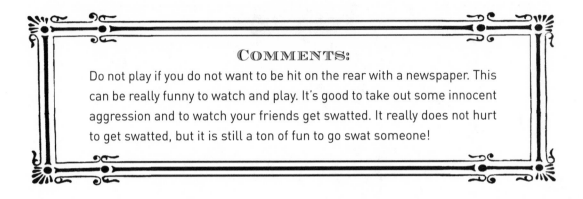

COMMENTS:

Do not play if you do not want to be hit on the rear with a newspaper. This can be really funny to watch and play. It's good to take out some innocent aggression and to watch your friends get swatted. It really does not hurt to get swatted, but it is still a ton of fun to go swat someone!

TEN BALL

NUMBER OF KIDS: at least 2

AGES: any

TIME ALLOTTED: 20 minutes or more

PLAYING FIELD: any large wall with a paved area in front

EQUIPMENT: 1 bouncy ball such as a tennis ball

START-UP: Players choose an order of players.

OBJECT: To complete all ten challenges.

PLAY: The first player begins with the ball and creates the first challenge. The challenge must include tossing the ball against the wall and catching it in the air or after one bounce. For example, the first player could say, "Hike the ball against the wall, turn around, and catch it in the air." Each player must then complete this challenge while saying, "One ball." If a player does not complete any challenge correctly, he or she is eliminated from the game. The next player then creates a different challenge. Players then must perform the first challenge and say, "One ball," and then perform the second challenge while saying, "Two ball." The next player then adds the third challenge and the process repeats. Every round, each player must perform each challenge in order, starting with the first one. This continues until ten challenges have been created and performed. Play continues until only one player is left or until ten challenges are completed. In the latter case, all players who complete the ten challenges win.

COMMENTS:

Creating the challenges is the best part of this game! Really be creative and try to outdo your opponents. Make difficult challenges, but remember that you have to complete them just like everyone else. Practice specialty tosses between games to help you win. It is a blast to watch your friends try all the crazy tricks and to try them yourself!

WHAT'S THE TIME, MR. WOLF?

NUMBER OF KIDS: 3 or more

AGES: any

TIME ALLOTTED: 20 minutes or more

PLAYING FIELD: a yard or large open, safe area

EQUIPMENT: none

START-UP: Players pick one person to be the wolf. A starting line is chosen about twenty feet behind the wolf where everyone else lines up. The wolf then faces away from the other players.

OBJECT: To get close to the wolf and not get caught.

PLAY: When everyone is set, the group calls out, "What's the time, Mr. Wolf?" The wolf then turns to the others and calls out a time (for example, five o'clock) and turns back around. The players then take that many steps toward the wolf (for example, if the wolf says, "five o'clock," then players take five steps). The wolf can look at the group only when he or she announces the time. The group again asks,

"What's the time, Mr. Wolf?" the wolf responds, and the group moves accordingly. This continues until the wolf senses that the group is close and instead of calling a time, the wolf says, "Dinner time!" and runs after all the other players. Whoever is caught by the wolf before getting back to the starting line is the next wolf. If no one is caught, the last person back to the line besides the wolf is the next wolf. Players can play as many rounds as desired.

COMMENTS:

This game is good for some startles. Be sneaky as the wolf. Don't wait until players get too close or else it is no fun, but try to take the players off guard and grab someone quickly. As players, try to get close to the wolf, and don't hide in the back. Take risks and have fun!

 # ACTIVITY LEVEL IV

BASE RUSH

NUMBER OF KIDS: at least 4

AGES: any

TIME ALLOTTED: 20 minutes or more

PLAYING FIELD: a long, open, grassy strip

EQUIPMENT: several identical objects that can serve as bases (such as Frisbees), 1 less than the number of children playing (e.g., 7 bases for 8 players)

START-UP: Players define a starting line and an ending line. The bases are then set up along the ending line. There should be one less base set up than there are players.

OBJECT: To be the last player remaining.

PLAY: Everyone lines up at the starting line. One player says, "Ready, set, go!" and everyone races for the end line. A player becomes safe by getting to and standing on one of the bases. No fighting for the bases is allowed; the first player there gets to stay on the base. Only one player can safely land on each base, so that one player will not find a base and is eliminated. One base is then removed and another round begins. This continues until there is only one player left, who is the winner.

COMMENTS:

This is a good game of speed, but some strategy is also involved in choosing which base to go for. It is like musical chairs with a lot more running. Good exercise, good competition, and clean fun!

BRITISH BULLDOG

NUMBER OF KIDS: at least 4

AGES: 8 and up

TIME ALLOTTED: 30 minutes or more

PLAYING FIELD: a large yard or open field

EQUIPMENT: none

START-UP: Players choose two lines for boundaries, about thirty or forty feet apart, and designate sidelines that cannot be crossed. Players also choose one player to be the bulldog. All players then line up on one side of the play area. The bulldog begins in the middle of the two lines.

OBJECT: To be the last person captured.

PLAY: The game begins when the bulldog yells, "British bulldog!" Everyone then attempts to cross the field to the other line without going out of bounds. While players cross, the bulldog tries to capture people and make them bulldogs also. The bulldog accomplishes this by lifting someone in the air while yelling, "One, two, three, British bulldog!" If the bulldog completes this successfully, the lifted person becomes a bulldog, too. Everyone who was safe lines up again and when everyone is ready, the bulldogs yell, "British bulldog!" and the process repeats. This continues until only one person is left uncaptured. This player is then the winner and the initial bulldog for the next round.

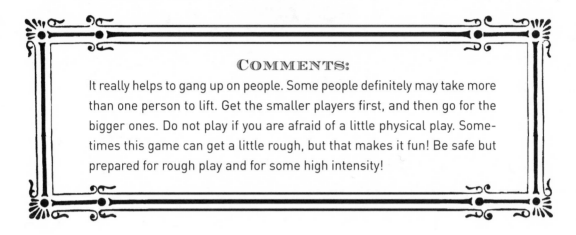

COMMENTS:

It really helps to gang up on people. Some people definitely may take more than one person to lift. Get the smaller players first, and then go for the bigger ones. Do not play if you are afraid of a little physical play. Sometimes this game can get a little rough, but that makes it fun! Be safe but prepared for rough play and for some high intensity!

CATEGORY TAG

NUMBER OF KIDS: at least 3

AGES: any

TIME ALLOTTED: 20 minutes or more

PLAYING FIELD: a small, grassy area

EQUIPMENT: none

START-UP: Players define small boundaries and choose someone to be It. A category for play is then chosen by the It and announced to all (for example, funny movies, actors, basketball players, types of fruit). Player should also decide if they need to be tagged once, twice, or three times to become It.

OBJECT: To avoid becoming It.

PLAY: Everyone spreads out in bounds. The It counts out loud to a certain number (usually 5 or 10) and the game begins. The It then attempts to tag everyone. The twist on this game is the category. A player may sit down safely until the It moves away if he or she is able to call out a member of the defined category. For example, if the category is sports, a player about to get tagged can yell out, "Basketball!" and sit down before he or she is tagged. For that player to be safe, the word must be yelled and the player must be on the ground before being tagged. Players cannot sit down until they have successfully called out the name. If a player successfully sits down, the It must chase someone else and the seated player must stand as quickly as possible. Once one player shouts out a member of the category, no other player can use that again. So the words must be yelled out so that all players can hear them. Once a player is tagged the decided number of times, that player becomes It, decides on a new category, and the game begins again.

An option is to play this game with no running at all.

COMMENTS:

Some may know this game as Sit-Down Tag. In this game, the It must be sure to run fast, because the faster he or she runs, the less time others have to think. This seems cheesy, but it is a thriller. Give it a try!

CATS IN THE CORNER

NUMBER OF KIDS: at least 4

AGES: any

TIME ALLOTTED: 45 minutes or more

PLAYING FIELD: a wide-open area where a square field can be defined

---

EQUIPMENT: 1 playground ball for every 4 players

START-UP: Players should define a large square field with four distinct corners. One out of every four people is chosen to be in the middle of the field. Each of these players starts with a ball and must stand in the center of the square. Everyone else is a cat, and all players go to the same corner to begin.

OBJECT: To be the last cat in the game (for cats), and to hit the most cats (for players in the middle).

PLAY: One of the players in the middle announces loudly, "Cats get a corner." The cats must then all run to the next corner in the counterclockwise direction. They can run fast or slow, individually or in a big group, but they all must run in the counterclockwise direction to the next corner. While the cats are between corners, the players in the middle try to hit them with the balls, but they must stay in the center of the square while throwing. While the cats are still in a corner, they cannot be hit. If a cat is hit with a ball, he or she is out and must go sit by the person who hit him or her. Once a ball is thrown, that ball cannot be thrown again until the next turn. Once all the cats have run and all the balls have been thrown, the balls are then retrieved by the throwers and they return to the middle. Once all the cats have safely arrived at the next corner or have been hit and seated, a player in the middle again announces, "Cats get a corner." The cats run to the next corner and the process repeats. This continues until only one cat is left. The last cat is the winner of the cats. The person in the middle who knocked out the most cats is the winner in the middle. Choose new players for the middle and begin again. If there are only enough players for one person to be in the middle, the last cat is the winner and begins the next round in the middle.

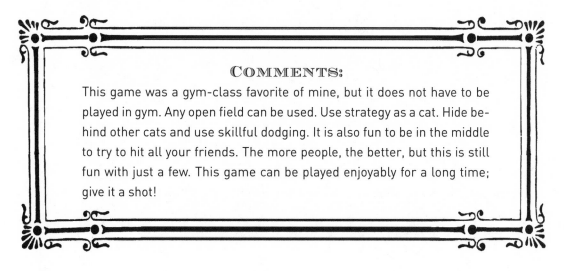

COMMENTS:

This game was a gym-class favorite of mine, but it does not have to be played in gym. Any open field can be used. Use strategy as a cat. Hide behind other cats and use skillful dodging. It is also fun to be in the middle to try to hit all your friends. The more people, the better, but this is still fun with just a few. This game can be played enjoyably for a long time; give it a shot!

CHICAGO

NUMBER OF KIDS: at least 2

AGES: 7 and up

TIME ALLOTTED: 30 minutes or more

PLAYING FIELD: any area with a basketball hoop

EQUIPMENT: 1 basketball

START-UP: Make sure the area has a marked free-throw line. Players decide who gets the ball first (by a shootout at the free-throw line if they want).

OBJECT: To be the first player to score twenty-one points.

PLAY: The game begins when the player with the ball checks it by passing the ball to another player and he or she passes it back. Each player then tries to score twenty-one points. Using basic basketball rules, if any player makes a basket, he or she earns two or three points accordingly. Fouls also apply, as in regular basketball. The trick to this game is that after a player makes a basket, he or she gets a chance to shoot free throws (each worth one point). If that player makes his or her first free throw, he or she keeps shooting, up to three times. If that player makes all three free throws, then he or she checks the ball and continues regular play. If that player misses a free throw, any player can get the rebound but then must dribble back to the three-point line and the game continues. This continues until one player reaches twenty-one points exactly. If a player goes over twenty-one, then that player's score returns to eleven and the game continues. The first player to reach exactly twenty-one points is the winner.

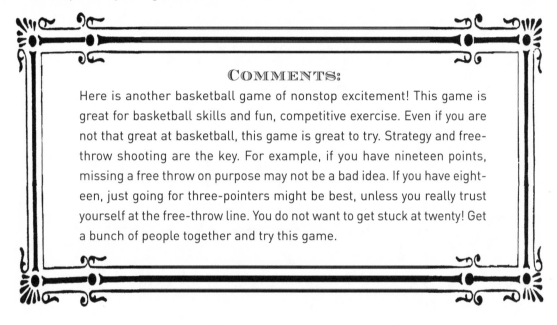

COMMENTS:

Here is another basketball game of nonstop excitement! This game is great for basketball skills and fun, competitive exercise. Even if you are not that great at basketball, this game is great to try. Strategy and free-throw shooting are the key. For example, if you have nineteen points, missing a free throw on purpose may not be a bad idea. If you have eighteen, just going for three-pointers might be best, unless you really trust yourself at the free-throw line. You do not want to get stuck at twenty! Get a bunch of people together and try this game.

CLUB BALL

NUMBER OF KIDS: at least 4

AGES: any

TIME ALLOTTED: 20 minutes or more

PLAYING FIELD: any open area

EQUIPMENT: 1 playground ball and 1 cone, bowling pin, large tin can, tennis ball can, or large plastic cup called the "club"

START-UP: Players should form a circular or square boundary and place the club in the middle. Players choose one person to be the first protector. The protector enters the playing boundaries with the ball. Everyone else gathers outside the boundary.

OBJECT: To knock over the club and be the protector.

PLAY: The protector starts the game by rolling the ball out of the playing area. Without entering the boundary, each player tries to obtain the ball. Then, by rolling the ball or kicking it softly, players try to knock over the club. The protector can do anything necessary within the boundaries to block the ball and keep it from knocking down the club. The protector cannot touch the club itself. If the ball is blocked or misses the club, another player grabs it and tries to knock over the club. Players are not allowed to enter the designated boundaries at any time. If the protector grabs the ball or if it stops inside the boundaries, the protector must toss it out to an outside player. If a player causes the club to fall, by hitting it with the ball or causing the protector to knock it over, then that player becomes the protector and a new round begins. If a player does this from inside the circle, it does not count; the club is set back up and play resumes.

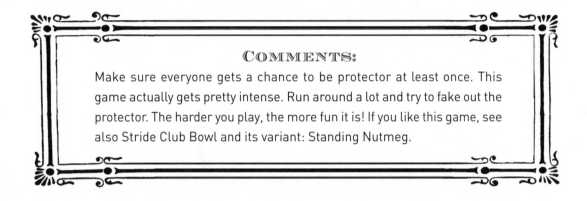

COMMENTS:

Make sure everyone gets a chance to be protector at least once. This game actually gets pretty intense. Run around a lot and try to fake out the protector. The harder you play, the more fun it is! If you like this game, see also Stride Club Bowl and its variant: Standing Nutmeg.

DARE GOAL

NUMBER OF KIDS: 2 teams of 3 or more

AGES: any

TIME ALLOTTED: 40 minutes or more

PLAYING FIELD: a large, open grassy area or field

EQUIPMENT: none

START-UP: Players should designate boundaries in a field that consist of two goal lines about sixty feet apart. Each goal line has a prison behind it. Players choose teams and each team selects a captain. The teams split up and each team goes to opposite goal lines.

OBJECT: To imprison all members of the other team.

PLAY: Everyone lines up along their goal line and the captain of one team chooses a challenger from his or her own team. This player walks across the field to the other team's goal line. Everyone on this team then holds out their right hand with their right elbow touching their side. The challenging player then walks down the line of the opposing team touching their outstretched hands. The challenging player may touch the hands in any order and may touch only the hands that he or she chooses. Whenever that player wishes, he or she slaps another player's hand fairly hard. The player whose hand was slapped becomes the chaser, and the challenger must run back to his or her goal line without being tagged by that player. If the challenger is successful, his or her team may choose to imprison the chaser or free an imprisoned member of their own team. If the challenger is tagged, the chaser's team gets to imprison the challenger. Being imprisoned means that player must stand in the other team's prison until he or she is freed or until the round ends. The other captain then selects a challenger and the same process occurs. This continues until one team has imprisoned all the members of the other team. The team who captures all the other players wins.

COMMENTS:

This is a great running and chasing game. Players have the fun of challenging one another and faking people out with phony slaps. This game promotes high-intensity action and can be fun for hours!

FOLLOW THE LEADER

NUMBER OF KIDS: at least 2

AGES: any

TIME ALLOTTED: 20 minutes or more

PLAYING FIELD: a playground or other safe area with various obstacles

---

EQUIPMENT: none

START-UP: Players choose someone to be the leader. Everyone forms a single-file line behind the leader.

OBJECT: To keep up with the leader, mimicking him or her as precisely as possible.

PLAY: There really are no stringent rules for this game. Once everyone is in line, the leader should do difficult physical tasks, such as climbing over objects or weaving through them. Every other player must follow and mimic the leader as closely as possible.

An optional rule, to add competition to the game, is when a player can be eliminated if he or she makes a mistake and does not follow the leader correctly. The last remaining player is the next leader. Otherwise, players can just take turns leading for a while. If players goof up, it is not a big deal; they just keep following as closely as they can. Play ends when everyone wants to stop.

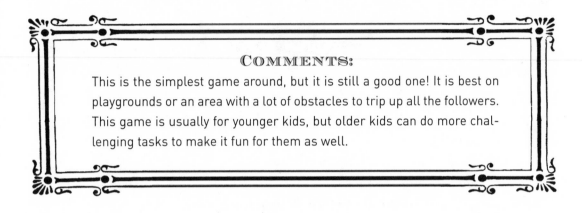

COMMENTS:

This is the simplest game around, but it is still a good one! It is best on playgrounds or an area with a lot of obstacles to trip up all the followers. This game is usually for younger kids, but older kids can do more challenging tasks to make it fun for them as well.

FOUR CORNERS

NUMBER OF KIDS: at least 5

AGES: any

TIME ALLOTTED: 20 minutes or more

PLAYING FIELD: a large square area where players can designate four corners or bases

EQUIPMENT: none

START-UP: Players should designate a large, square playing area with four corners or bases. One player is picked as the caller at the beginning of each game. The caller stands out of bounds for the entire round. Everyone else gets into the middle of the square.

OBJECT: To be the last player in the game.

PLAY: Rules are picked for each of the four corners. Four standard rules are the following:

• Corner 1: The last person to get to the corner and sit down is out.

- Corner 2: Each player must get to the corner, hold hands with one partner, and sit down. The person left with no partner is out or the last pair to sit down is out.

- Corner 3: Same rule as for corner 2, but players form groups of three.

- Corner 4: Players run to the corner, spin around ten times, and then sit down. The last person to do so is out.

The great part about this game is that the rules can be easily changed if desired. Players can have fun making up crazy rules for each corner. The important thing is to make sure that everyone knows which corners are 1, 2, 3, and 4, and which rule applies to which corner. Once the rules are determined, the players all get together in the middle and the caller yells out a number (1, 2, 3, or 4). Everyone but the caller rushes to that corner and follows the rule that applies. Whoever is eliminated moves out of bounds and waits for the next round. Everyone else moves back into the center and the caller yells out a corner and the process repeats itself. The last person left is the winner and becomes the caller for the next game.

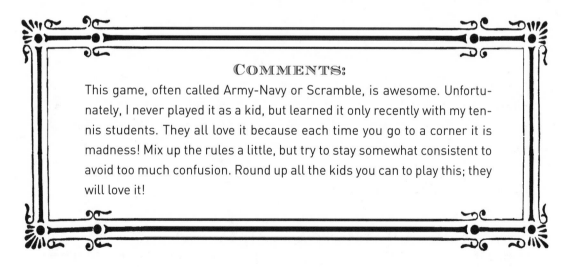

COMMENTS:

This game, often called Army-Navy or Scramble, is awesome. Unfortunately, I never played it as a kid, but learned it only recently with my tennis students. They all love it because each time you go to a corner it is madness! Mix up the rules a little, but try to stay somewhat consistent to avoid too much confusion. Round up all the kids you can to play this; they will love it!

FOX AND GEESE

NUMBER OF KIDS: at least 2

AGES: any

TIME ALLOTTED: 15 minutes or more

PLAYING FIELD: a large paved area that can be drawn on with chalk

EQUIPMENT: 1 piece of chalk

START-UP: One player should draw a large circle with chalk that has four evenly spaced lines running through it, so that it looks likes a sliced pizza. One player is chosen to be the fox. The fox stands is the center of the circle. Everyone else, the geese, spreads out on the circle.

OBJECT: To avoid being the fox.

PLAY: The fox counts out loud to three and the game begins. A game of tag with some twists is then played. All players, including the fox, must remain on the drawn lines. Players may go around the circle or through it on any drawn line. If a player is tagged or does not stay on the lines, that player becomes the fox. He or she then pauses, counts aloud to three, and the game continues. Play continues for as long as players want.

If players play on a smaller playing field, running should not be allowed. This will stop players from flying off the lines.

COMMENTS:

This is a great version of tag. It is challenging to stay on the lines when being chased. Also, watch out for people walking toward you on your line because it is very difficult to pass someone without stepping off the lines. Try it and see for yourself!

FREEZE TAG

NUMBER OF KIDS: at least 3

AGES: any

TIME ALLOTTED: 20 minutes or more

PLAYING FIELD: a yard or large grassy area

EQUIPMENT: none

START-UP: Players should define boundaries and choose someone to be It.

OBJECT: To avoid being It.

PLAY: Everyone spreads out in bounds. The player who is It counts out loud to a certain number and the game begins. The It then attempts to tag everyone. If a player is tagged, that player must freeze where he or she was tagged. A player automatically becomes unfrozen as soon as any other player (except the It) touches him or her in any way. The round ends when one person has been tagged three times, or when the It has frozen everyone. In the event that a player is tagged three times, that player is It the next round. If the It manages to freeze everyone (a rarity), the round ends and the current It chooses the next It.

Variant:

TUNNEL TAG: This game is similar, except when a player gets tagged, that player must stand in place with his or her legs spread. Players are only unfrozen when another player crawls through their legs. If a player is tagged halfway through someone's legs, the player that was frozen is freed and the tagged player is then frozen in that spot. All other rules apply.

HIT OR RUN

NUMBER OF KIDS: at least 7, or 6 and 1 adult

AGES: any

TIME ALLOTTED: 30 minutes or more

PLAYING FIELD: any large open yard or field

EQUIPMENT: 2 playground balls

START-UP: Players should designate two lines on either end of the field, and a box in the middle that extends across the field. Players also place the two balls in the middle of the box and choose two teams. One person is designated to call numbers. The caller then assigns numbers, starting with one and counting up, to the players on each team so there is one person on each team with each number. Each team proceeds to opposing ends of the field. The caller remains on the side of the field.

OBJECT: To be on the first team to get ten points. A higher number of points can be used (perhaps 15 or 20) if there are larger numbers of children.

PLAY: The caller yells out a number of a player. The two players with that number run toward the middle box. The object is for one player to grab a ball and return it to his or her sideline safely. There are two options in this game, however, once a player grabs a ball. Once a player leaves the center box with a ball, he or she can be hit by the other player's ball. A player with a ball can either run back to his or her own sideline or try to hit the other player with the ball. A player cannot be hit until he or she has left the center box with a ball. Any throw must come from within the center box. If a player is hit, the team of the player who threw the ball gets a point. If no one gets hit, it is simply the first player who crosses his or her goal line with a ball earns a point. After a point is earned, the players return and repeat the process. The game is over once a team reaches ten points.

COMMENTS:

This game requires high intensity and is exciting to play. Be risky but safe at the same time. Try to grab your ball fast so you have the decision to break for it or begin a showdown. This is a little more oriented toward older kids, but anyone can play. The caller should try to give everyone an equal turn to try to break for the middle.

HOT BOX

Number of kids: at least 4

Ages: 6 and up

Time allotted: 30 minutes or more

Playing field: a wide, grassy strip at least 20 feet long, or any large, open grassy area

---

Equipment: 2 bases (such as Frisbees) and 1 ball to toss (such as a tennis ball), or 2 gloves and 1 baseball or softball. For a large number of players, choose larger bases (such as old towels) so there is enough room for everyone to have at least one foot touching.

Start-up: The bases are set up about twenty to thirty feet apart. Two people are chosen to be the throwers. Everyone else is a runner.

Object: To not get tagged (for runners) and to tag or hit the runners (for throwers).

Play: Each thrower stands in front of one base. The runners split up and get on one of the two bases. The throwers begin by tossing the ball back and forth. The runners then attempt to run back and forth between the bases anytime they feel they can do so without getting tagged. Whenever the runners are off base, the throwers try to tag them with the ball or hit them with it (which is only allowed if a softball is chosen). If a baseball or soft ball and gloves are used, only tagging with the glove is allowed. Each time a runner is tagged off base, one point is added to that player's tally. If a runner is tagged off base a certain number of times (usually three), that runner becomes the thrower and the person who has been throwing for the longest time becomes a runner. For the first switch, whoever tagged the runner last is the one who switches. After each switch, every runner's tally (number of times tagged) remains the same, and the game continues as before. The game ends whenever the players want to stop.

COMMENTS:

This game is great and is a childhood favorite of mine. Play this one! Take risks while playing! The more risks the runners take, the more fun it is to run. If you are throwing, mix up the throws to lure people off base: throw high balls, grounders, or drop the ball on purpose. Everybody will like this game!

INFILTRATION

NUMBER OF KIDS: 2 teams of 4 or more

AGES: any

TIME ALLOTTED: at least 1 hour

PLAYING FIELD: a large field with some obstacles (best at night or dusk)

EQUIPMENT: 2 flashlights

START-UP: Players should define rectangular boundaries around a field about 100 yards long and fairly wide. A middle line is then defined on the field. Two teams are formed and one player from each team is assigned to be a guard. The guards each get a flashlight. The guards remain on the middle line while each team goes to opposite ends of the field.

OBJECT: To score ten points first.

PLAY: When everyone is in position, the guards announce "Go!" and the game begins. Players try to cross the middle line without getting spotted by the guard of the other team. Players can travel by any means (such as crawling or running). The guards try to shine their flashlights on the incoming opponents but should not keep their flashlights on all the time. If the guards spot someone, the guard announces "You're caught!" loudly and that person has to start over at his or her end of the field. If a player successfully passes the middle line without being spotted, that player yells, "Infiltration!" loudly and his or her team earns one point. That player must then go back to his or her end of the field to try to score again. Play does not stop when someone scores but it is always going on. The first team to earn ten points wins. Choose new guards or mix up teams and play again!

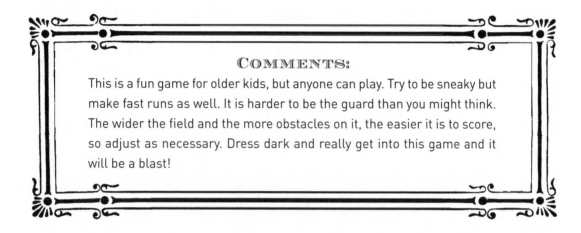

COMMENTS:

This is a fun game for older kids, but anyone can play. Try to be sneaky but make fast runs as well. It is harder to be the guard than you might think. The wider the field and the more obstacles on it, the easier it is to score, so adjust as necessary. Dress dark and really get into this game and it will be a blast!

KNOCKOUT

NUMBER OF KIDS: at least 4

AGES: any

TIME ALLOTTED: 15 minutes or more

PLAYING FIELD: any area with a basketball hoop

EQUIPMENT: 2 basketballs

START-UP: Players choose an order and get in a single-file line beginning at the foul line. The first two players each get one ball.

OBJECT: To be the last player remaining.

PLAY: The first player in line shoots the ball, trying to make a basket. After the first player shoots, the second player shoots, trying to make a basket. If any player misses the shot, he or she must rebound the ball and make a basket with it from any location, even a lay-up. When a player makes his or her shot, that player must get the rebound and pass the ball to whoever is currently next in line. The first shot from every player must come from the foul line. The trick is that two players are always trying to make a basket at the same time. Whichever player is ahead in the order must make the basket first. If at any point a player makes a basket before the person in front of him or her, the player who didn't make the basket in time is knocked out of the game. The game is then paused, the balls are given to the next two players in line, and it all begins again. The last player left at the end is the winner.

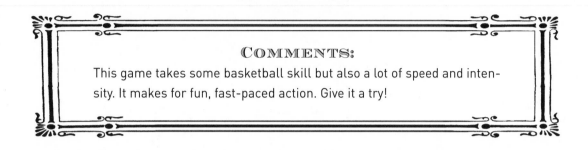

COMMENTS:

This game takes some basketball skill but also a lot of speed and intensity. It makes for fun, fast-paced action. Give it a try!

LAST MAN TAG

NUMBER OF KIDS: 2 teams of 3 or more

AGES: any

TIME ALLOTTED: at least 45 minutes

PLAYING FIELD: a large, open grassy area

EQUIPMENT: none

START-UP: Players should define boundaries that consist of two large bases, located about fifty feet apart. Teams are chosen and each team goes to opposing bases.

OBJECT: To eliminate all the players on the other team.

PLAY: Once players are on their bases, someone yells "Go!" and the game begins. Players can then leave base at any time, but once a player is off the base, he or she may be tagged by an opposing player. The trick is that to be able to tag an opponent, the tagger must have left the base after his or her opponent left base (this sounds complicated, but it is simple when put into play). Players are safe by returning to base or by successfully making a tag. Any tagged player is eliminated from the game. A successful tagger is temporarily safe but must return to his or her base immediately (to indicate a safe return, a player should hold both hands in the air while running back to base). Upon reaching base, the tagger can then attempt another tag but is unsafe again as soon as he or she leaves base. Play does not stop when a tag is made. Play is continuous and tagging can occur anytime a player is not safe. Play continues until one team has had all their players eliminated.

COMMENTS:

Players should both lure out their opponents and aggressively try to tag. You would not believe how much fun this can be! Do not hide on base all day. The more time you spend in the playing area trying to lure others off base or trying to tag someone, the more fun it is. Be aggressive and risky and have fun! Go try this game!

LINK TAG

NUMBER OF KIDS: at least 6

AGES: any

TIME ALLOTTED: at least 20 minutes

PLAYING FIELD: a yard or large open area

EQUIPMENT: none

START-UP: Players should define boundaries and choose a chaser and a runner. Everyone else then finds a partner. The pairs should spread out in bounds and stand with their elbows linked together.

OBJECT: To avoid being the chaser.

PLAY: Everyone spreads out in bounds. The chaser counts out loud to a certain number and the game begins. The chaser is always in pursuit of the runner. If the runner is tagged, he or she then becomes the chaser and the chaser becomes the runner. At any time, the runner can link elbows with someone. If the runner links with a pair of people, the person on the other side of that linked duo must break off and become the runner. A runner can be chased as long as he or she wants before linking up. Tag-backs are allowed, which means that if the chaser tags the runner, the two immediately trade places and the game continues. The game ends when everyone decides to quit.

An option is that if someone is watching or wants to sit out, that person can be given the power to call "switch" at any time. When switch is called, the runner immediately becomes the chaser and vice versa. This is especially advisable with an odd number of players. With an odd number of players, another option is to play with two runners.

COMMENTS:

This game is fun for a little chaos, but it is very safe and enjoyable. Switching is hilarious to watch if you use it, but this game is always a wild time!

MULBERRY BUSH

NUMBER OF KIDS: at least 2

AGES: any

TIME ALLOTTED: 10 minutes or more

PLAYING FIELD: any small open area

EQUIPMENT: none

START-UP: Everyone forms a circle. Players may circle around an object (such as a bush) if desired.

OBJECT: To enjoy the game.

PLAY: Players began to skip around in a circle while chanting. The first lyrics chanted are, "Here we go round the mulberry bush, the mulberry bush, the mulberry bush. Here we go round the mulberry bush, so early in the morning." Players continue to skip around the circle while singing the next verses. The succeeding verses are based on daily activities. For example, "This is the way we brush our teeth, brush our teeth, brush our teeth. This is the way we brush our teeth, so early in the morning." Players should take turns naming the activity to sing. Other common verses include washing clothes, ironing clothes, sweeping the floor, eating food, and getting dressed, but anything can be used. Players should also act out the action while skipping and singing. For example, while singing about brushing teeth, players should pretend to brush their teeth while they skip and sing.

COMMENTS:

An enjoyable, easy game, that little children and anyone else can play. A true classic that is good, clean fun.

NO TOUCH GROUND

NUMBER OF KIDS: 1 or more

AGES: any

TIME ALLOTTED: 20 minutes or more

PLAYING FIELD: a playground or a safe area with many obstacles

---

EQUIPMENT: none

START-UP: One player chooses a starting point and a destination.

OBJECT: To reach the chosen destination without touching the ground.

PLAY: There are not too many rules in this game except for not touching the ground. Players attempt to go from the starting point to the destination without touching the ground at all, or at least as little as possible. Players should attempt to stay on top of obstacles or the playground equipment as they make their way to the destination. The player that chose the destination usually starts off, and the others follow or make their own path. When everyone reaches the destination, have a new player choose another destination and proceed as before.

If competition is desired, a rule can be applied where any player who does touch the ground accidentally is eliminated. Whoever gets closest to the destination without touching ground is the winner and chooses the next destination. If multiple players complete the course, they are all winners.

An optional rule is for players to take turns being the leader instead of having an end destination. The leader should then move around the playground or area without touching the ground and the other players must do what the leader does. If players touch the ground or fail to follow the leader, they are eliminated. If the leader touches the ground, a new leader is chosen and the game continues.

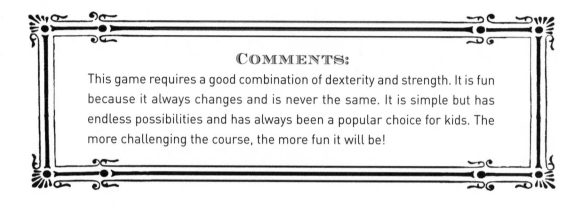

COMMENTS:

This game requires a good combination of dexterity and strength. It is fun because it always changes and is never the same. It is simple but has endless possibilities and has always been a popular choice for kids. The more challenging the course, the more fun it will be!

RED LIGHT, GREEN LIGHT

NUMBER OF KIDS: 3 or more

AGES: any

TIME ALLOTTED: 20 minutes or more

PLAYING FIELD: a straight path on any surface

EQUIPMENT: none

START-UP: Players should choose a starting line and then pick someone to be It. The It walks back from the starting line as far as he or she sees fit. Everyone else lines up on the starting line.

OBJECT: To be the first player to reach the It.

PLAY: The game begins when the It calls out "green light." At that point, everyone advances toward the It as fast as possible. When the It calls out "red light," everyone must stop immediately. Those who do not stop right away are forced to move back as far as the It deems necessary. The It then calls out "green light" again and everyone begins to run until the It calls out "red light." This repeats until one player reaches and tags the It. This player is the winner and becomes It for the next round.

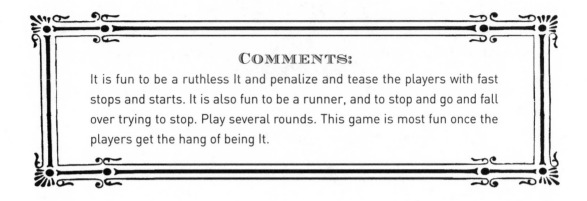

COMMENTS:

It is fun to be a ruthless It and penalize and tease the players with fast stops and starts. It is also fun to be a runner, and to stop and go and fall over trying to stop. Play several rounds. This game is most fun once the players get the hang of being It.

RELAYS

NUMBER OF KIDS: at least 2 teams of 2 or more

AGES: usually any, depends on relay

TIME ALLOTTED: 20 minutes or more

PLAYING FIELD: depends on relay chosen

EQUIPMENT: depends on relay chosen

START-UP: Players should choose a type of relay and teams are chosen accordingly.

OBJECT: To win the relay by finishing first or the fastest.

PLAY: A list of all possible relays would be far too extensive because any simple task may be turned into a relay. An example is placing four balls in a large square pattern. The first person must pick up all four balls, one at a time, and hand them to the next person in line. That second person then must put them back one at a time, returning to the starting point after setting down each ball. After each player has gone once, the team who finishes first wins.

Bike races around blocks, dribbling tennis balls up and down a driveway, climbing around a jungle gym, and throwing a Frisbee down three yards and back were all fun ideas we used to do. Also, any sort of funny body position or teamwork task can be used. Teams can race all at once or can take turns and time each other. Whoever finishes the relay first or fastest is the winner. The winning team can pick the next type of relay.

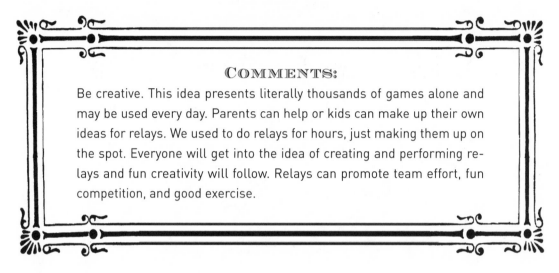

COMMENTS:

Be creative. This idea presents literally thousands of games alone and may be used every day. Parents can help or kids can make up their own ideas for relays. We used to do relays for hours, just making them up on the spot. Everyone will get into the idea of creating and performing relays and fun creativity will follow. Relays can promote team effort, fun competition, and good exercise.

RIM GAME

NUMBER OF KIDS: 2 or more

AGES: 7 or older

TIME ALLOTTED: 40 minutes or more

PLAYING FIELD: any basketball hoop

EQUIPMENT: 1 basketball and 1 piece of chalk if no foul box is present

START-UP: If there is no foul box, a box must be drawn with chalk on the ground of about the same size. If a driveway has squares in its design, that can also work well. The foul box creates the boundaries. Players then choose a shooting order.

OBJECT: To give others points while keeping one's own points to a minimum.

PLAY: The first player starts on the foul line (or end of the box) and tosses the basketball so that it hits the rim of the basketball hoop. The next player must then gain possession of the ball. This player then moves around freely within the designated box. The player with the ball does not have to dribble, and the other players do not guard him or her. While staying anywhere in bounds, he or she then throws the ball against any part of the rim, in any style chosen. The next player then catches the ball and repeats the process, and so on.

The trick of the game comes with the narrower rules and point scoring. After the ball is thrown by a player, it must strike some part of the rim (backboard alone does not count), and the ball must land within bounds. If the ball misses the rim and lands out of bounds or lands out of bounds after hitting the rim, the player who threw the ball out of bounds (off the rim or not) loses the point and that point is added to the player's tally of lost points.

If the ball does land in bounds after hitting the rim, it is then the next person's turn. The next player must catch the ball before it goes out of bounds. He or she can catch the ball before or after it bounces but must not step out of bounds, as in regular basketball. A jumping save may be made as long as the ball never lands out of bounds and as long as the player never touches the ball while he or she is out of bounds. If a save is made, the player still must obtain possession of the ball before it goes back out of the box. If a fair ball does go out of bounds or an illegal save is made when it becomes someone's turn, that player loses the point. It remains a player's turn until that player successfully catches and throws the ball against the rim of the basket. It then becomes the next person's turn, and so on. Whenever a point is lost, play stops, and the next player in order begins a new point at the foul line as before. A player is eliminated when he or she loses five or ten points (determined at the start). Play continues until only one player is left.

Interference with another player or his or her ball is never allowed. If it does happen, a redo can be declared. Players must do their best to avoid the ball when it is not their turn. An optional rule may even be played where the point is lost by a player if the ball strikes that player when it is not his or her turn.

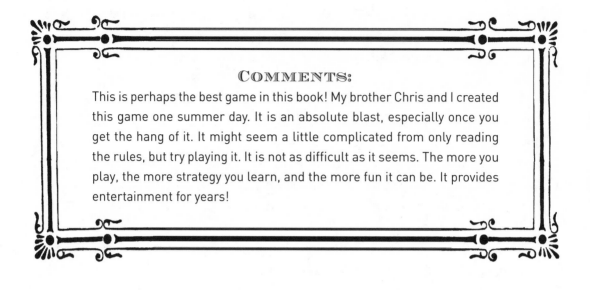

COMMENTS:

This is perhaps the best game in this book! My brother Chris and I created this game one summer day. It is an absolute blast, especially once you get the hang of it. It might seem a little complicated from only reading the rules, but try playing it. It is not as difficult as it seems. The more you play, the more strategy you learn, and the more fun it can be. It provides entertainment for years!

ROOF GAME

NUMBER OF KIDS: 2 or more (divide into teams with 4 or more)

AGES: any

TIME ALLOTTED: 15 minutes or more

PLAYING FIELD: a slanted roof with no gutter that has room to run in front of it (a roof with a gutter can be used with a large, soft ball that will not get caught in or damage the gutter)

EQUIPMENT: 1 bouncy ball, such as a tennis ball

START-UP: The trick is finding a good roof that works. Players then choose an order if there are more than two players or teams. Players should also define boundaries on the roof if it is more than twenty feet long.

OBJECT: To give others points while keeping one's own points to a minimum.

PLAY: The person who is first in order gets the ball and tosses it onto the roof from anywhere in any manner chosen (such as high and bouncy, or low and hard). The ball must land on the roof and roll off the front of the roof (not off one of the sides or out of the designated area). An illegal throw causes the thrower to lose a point. Every time a legal throw is made, the next player must catch the ball before it hits the ground. If the ball is caught, that player throws it onto the roof for the next player to catch. If the ball is dropped, the player who was supposed to catch it loses a point and that is added to that player's tally of points lost. A player is eliminated upon reaching five points. A new game can then be started or play can continue until only one player is left.

COMMENTS:

Unlike what you might think, the trick to this game is not in the catching but in the throwing. Try throwing the ball with spins or bounces that make it difficult to catch, or perhaps throw it so it barely touches the top of the roof and then falls down. This is a very simple game for all ages, but do not let its simplicity fool you. It is surprisingly challenging and exciting!

SPINNING ROPE

NUMBER OF KIDS: at least 3

AGES: any

TIME ALLOTTED: 15 minutes or more

PLAYING FIELD: a large paved or hard and smooth surface

EQUIPMENT: 1 long jump rope (or a rope with a small weight on one end)

START-UP: Players choose someone to be It and he or she starts in the middle of the others, holding one end of the rope. The other players line up around the It, staying within the length of the rope.

OBJECT: Not to get hit by the rope.

PLAY: The It grabs one end of the rope and begins spinning so that the rope also spins along the ground (not in the air) in a big circle. The other players must jump the rope without it touching them. The It may slow down, speed up, move the rope up and down a little, and so on, to try to get the jumpers hit by the rope. When a player is hit by the rope, he or she becomes the new It and play continues. The game ends whenever the players agree to stop.

COMMENTS:

This is a simple game but it makes for a good time, especially with kids of mixed ages.

SPRITE BALL

NUMBER OF KIDS: at least 5

AGES: any

TIME ALLOTTED: 40 minutes or more

PLAYING FIELD: any large, open area

EQUIPMENT: 1 playground ball

START-UP: Players should choose someone to be It and define a square field with two distinct end lines and a center area for the It to stand in. The It stands in the middle area and everyone else splits evenly behind the two end lines of the field.

OBJECT: To avoid becoming It.

PLAY: Once everyone is ready, the It announces a player's name. That player then calls out the name of a player on the opposing end line. These players must instantly step across the end line into bounds. They then trade places by crossing to the other side of the field. Without leaving the center circle, the It tries to hit either of the two players with the ball as they cross the field. Players can run anywhere in bounds to try to dodge the ball. If a player is hit with the ball, he or she becomes It for the next round. If both players cross successfully, the It remains in place and another round begins.

If there are many players, an optional rule can be used where the It can call two or even three players from each line. This rule adds a little more excitement and strategy to the game.

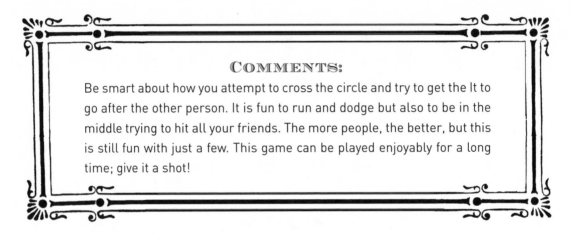

COMMENTS:

Be smart about how you attempt to cross the circle and try to get the It to go after the other person. It is fun to run and dodge but also to be in the middle trying to hit all your friends. The more people, the better, but this is still fun with just a few. This game can be played enjoyably for a long time; give it a shot!

STATUES

NUMBER OF KIDS: 3 or more

AGES: any

TIME ALLOTTED: 20 minutes or more

PLAYING FIELD: a large grassy, open area

EQUIPMENT: none

START-UP: Players should define boundaries and choose a judge.

OBJECT: To be the last player in the game.

PLAY: Everyone but the judge begins to move about randomly within the defined area. The judge yells, "Freeze!" at will, whereupon everyone must freeze instantly like statues. Failing to freeze instantly results in elimination from the game. The players must hold their position until approved by the judge. The judge walks around and asks what each statue is posing as. If an acceptable answer is given by all the players and no one falls, "Unfreeze!" is called out by the judge and everyone begins to move again. If anyone falls, cannot hold their statue position, or the judge does not think that an answer justifies the pose, that player is eliminated. The judge is responsible for all elimination decisions. The last person remaining wins and is judge for the next round.

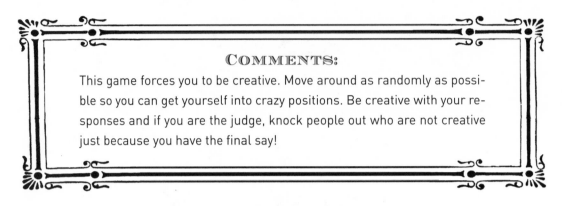

COMMENTS:

This game forces you to be creative. Move around as randomly as possible so you can get yourself into crazy positions. Be creative with your responses and if you are the judge, knock people out who are not creative just because you have the final say!

Variant:

RED LIGHT, GREEN LIGHT STATUES: This variant adds an important rule to Red Light, Green Light. When "red light" is called out, everyone must stop immediately and hold their position as statues. If a player moves before "green light" is called, then that player must start over at the beginning (but is not eliminated). Each person must also call out what they are posing as in their statue position. The It, or the judge, may make a player start over for a bad answer as well. Then "green light" is called again and play continues. All the other rules of Red Light, Green Light apply.

STEAL THE BACON

NUMBER OF KIDS: at least 7, or 6 and 1 adult

AGES: any

TIME ALLOTTED: 30 minutes or more

PLAYING FIELD: a large open yard, field, or paved area

EQUIPMENT: 1 item to be grabbed, such as a handkerchief or piece of rope

START-UP: Players should designate two lines, separated by the playing field, and place the "bacon" in the middle. Players also choose two teams and designate another player to call out numbers. The caller then assigns a number, starting with one, to the players on each team. Each team proceeds to opposing ends of the field. The caller remains on the side of the field.

OBJECT: To be the first team to get ten points. A higher number of points can be used (perhaps 15 or 20) if there are larger numbers of children.

PLAY: Once everyone is ready, the caller yells out a players' number. There should be one person on each team with that number. These two players run toward the bacon. The object is for one player to grab the bacon and return it to his or her sideline without being tagged by the other player. Either player can grab the bacon but a player doesn't have to grab it. A player can wait for the opponent to grab the bacon and try for the tag. A player cannot be tagged until he or she grabs the bacon. If a player grabs the bacon and makes it back to his or her line without being tagged, that team earns a point. If the player is tagged before making it back, the tagger's team scores the point. Once the bacon is grabbed, it cannot be dropped. If it is dropped, the player attempting the tag earns the point. After a team earns a point, the bacon is placed back in the middle, the players return to their side, and the caller calls another number. The first team to reach ten points is the winner.

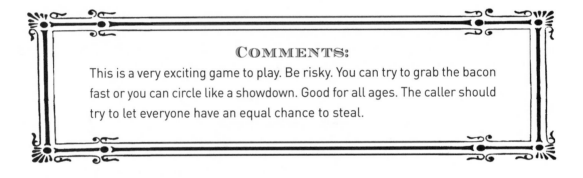

COMMENTS:

This is a very exciting game to play. Be risky. You can try to grab the bacon fast or you can circle like a showdown. Good for all ages. The caller should try to let everyone have an equal chance to steal.

STRIDE CLUB BOWL

NUMBER OF KIDS: at least 4

AGES: any

TIME ALLOTTED: 20 minutes or more

PLAYING FIELD: any open area

EQUIPMENT: 1 or more playground balls (depending on the number of players) and 1 cone, bowling pin, tennis ball can, large tin can, or large plastic cup called the "club" for each player

START-UP: Everyone stands in a circle with their feet spread wide apart. The circle should be formed with everyone's feet touching toe-to-toe with the person next to him or her. Each player places his or her club directly between his or her feet.

OBJECT: To be the last remaining player.

PLAY: The ball or balls are given to a player at random. One player says, "Ready, set, go!" and the game begins. Pushing and shoving are not allowed. Moving one's foot and throwing the ball are also not allowed. Otherwise, players can do whatever they can to knock over their opponents' club with a ball. Players should also be sure to protect their own club. The ball must be rolled or pushed through the hands of a player to knock down the club. If a player's club is knocked over or a player moves his or her feet without getting pushed, that player is eliminated. Only one player can be eliminated at a time. If two pins are knocked down close together, only the player whose pin was knocked over first is out. As soon as one player is eliminated, the game is paused and a smaller circle is formed in the same fashion. The player who caused the elimination begins with the ball and says, "Ready, set, go!" The whole process repeats and continues until only one player is left. That player is the winner and begins with the ball the next round.

COMMENTS:

You don't run much in this game, but it will wear you out faster than you think. It is very intense, stressful, and fun at the same time! This is a different type of game then most people have played and is a riot to try.

If you like this, see also Club Ball and try the variants!

Variant:

STANDING NUTMEG: If no cones are available, try this version. The rules are the same except players must roll or shove the ball all the way through another player's legs to eliminate them instead of knocking over the opponent's club.

Variant:

BROOKLYN BRIDGE: This game is similar to Standing Nutmeg except players form two teams. The teams get into a two lines facing each other and play team Standing Nutmeg. As players are eliminated, their team's line slides together to close the gap. The team with the last player(s) is the winner.

TIGER AND LEOPARD

NUMBER OF KIDS: at least 2

AGES: any

TIME ALLOTTED: 15 minutes or more

PLAYING FIELD: any open field

EQUIPMENT: none

START-UP: Players should choose a starting line and a finish line, and divide into groups of tigers and leopards. There should be a few more tigers than leopards.

OBJECT: To be a leopard.

PLAY: Tigers line up on the starting line facing the finish line. Leopards stand behind the tigers and chant, "A tiger, a leopard, a tiger, a leopard, one of them crouches, the other leaps over." Upon hearing "one of them crouches," the tigers crouch all the way down. After finishing the chant, the leopards leap over any chosen tiger. The tigers that were leaped over must then chase and tag the leopard who jumped over them. If the leopard crosses the finish line without being tagged, he or she remains a leopard. If a leopard is tagged, the tiger who tagged him or her becomes a leopard and the tagged leopard becomes a tiger. Players can play as many rounds as they desire.

COMMENTS:

This is a great game of tag, chase, and leapfrog combined into one. It makes for tons of exercise and a lot of fun.

TWO-PERSON BASKETBALL

NUMBER OF KIDS: 2 teams of at least 3

AGES: any

TIME ALLOTTED: 30 minutes or more

PLAYING FIELD: half of a basketball court

EQUIPMENT: 1 basketball

START-UP: Players should choose two teams and designate one person to call numbers. The caller then assigns a number, starting with one, to the players on each team. The teams then proceed to opposing sidelines of the chosen half of the basketball court.

OBJECT: To be on the first team to get ten points.

PLAY: When everyone is ready, the caller yells out one or two numbers (of the caller's choice). There should be a person on each team with the number(s). As the caller yells the numbers, he or she bounces the basketball off the backboard hard and the point begins. The players who were called run to get possession of the ball and score. The first player or team to score gets the point for his or her team. Normal basketball rules apply (no pushing, no hacking, no double dribbling, no traveling, and so on) except that everyone tries to score on the same basket. After a score is made, the players return to their sidelines, the caller calls another number and the process repeats. This continues until one team scores ten points and wins. After each game, a new person should be made caller.

If there is an even number of players, the ball can be set in the middle of the foul line and one player from each team can take turns calling the numbers.

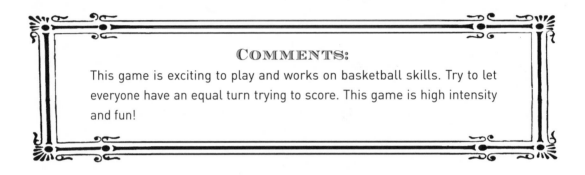

COMMENTS:
This game is exciting to play and works on basketball skills. Try to let everyone have an equal turn trying to score. This game is high intensity and fun!

WALL BALL

NUMBER OF KIDS: 2 or more

AGES: 6 and up

TIME ALLOTTED: 25 minutes or more

PLAYING FIELD: any large wall with a paved area in front

EQUIPMENT: 1 bouncy ball such as a tennis ball

START-UP: Players should find a good, open wall and set boundaries on the pavement. Boundaries should be about ten feet wide and fifteen feet long. If there are more than two players, they must choose an order.

OBJECT: To give others points while keeping one's own points to a minimum.

PLAY: The first person begins by tossing the ball against the wall from anywhere he or she chooses. The trick is that after hitting the wall, the ball must land on the pavement within the designated boundaries. The next person must then catch the ball after one bounce or in the air. That player then throws the ball against the wall and the next person must catch it. If at any time the ball bounces twice on a fair throw, the player who is attempting to catch the ball loses the point. If one loses a point, that player adds one point to his or her tally of lost points. If a throw bounces off the wall and lands out of bounds, the thrower gets the point. When five or ten points is reached by one player, that player is out of the game. The last person left is the winner.

COMMENTS:

This game was a childhood and a teenage favorite. It sounds simple, but it can be a lot more fun and complex than you might imagine. This is a simple, relatively unstructured game that is good for just goofing around with friends. If played seriously, it can also be high intensity with lots of funny incidents and skilled points. Definitely worth a try!

ACTIVITY
LEVEL V

BALL TAG

NUMBER OF KIDS: 2 or more

AGES: any

TIME ALLOTTED: 15 minutes or more

PLAYING FIELD: a grassy area or yard, preferably with some obstacles

---

EQUIPMENT: 1 soft ball, such as a playground or beach ball

START-UP: Players should select a ball, define boundaries, and choose someone to be It.

OBJECT: To avoid being It.

PLAY: Everyone spreads out in bounds. The player who is It counts out loud to a certain number and the game begins. The It then attempts to hit anyone with the ball. If the It is successful in hitting another player with the ball, that player becomes the It and play continues. Players may run and dodge the ball in any way they choose. They may also catch the ball to avoid becoming it. If the ball is caught, it is set on the ground, the It must go get the ball, and play resumes. The game continues for as long as the players want.

COMMENTS:

This game is a classic, simple and fun. It might seem dull, but it can be very intense. Once kids get into it, this game can provide quality enter-tainment for a good amount of time!

BALLOON VOLLEY

NUMBER OF KIDS: 2 teams of 2 or more; or 1 on 1

AGES: any

TIME ALLOTTED: 30 minutes or more

PLAYING FIELD: a large open field

EQUIPMENT: 1 or more air-filled balloons (depending on the number of players)

START-UP: Players should define a playing field with goal lines on each end and choose teams. They should then choose how many points must be scored to win the game.

OBJECT: To score points by hitting the balloon(s) over the opponent's goal line.

PLAY: Each team scatters in the field as desired. The balloon or balloons are tossed into the air in the middle of the field and play begins. Players must never catch or hold the balloon, but they can bat or kick it in any other way. A player or team scores one point for hitting a balloon over the opponent's goal line. No rough play or physical contact is allowed. Play continues until each balloon has been hit over a goal line. Then all balloons are brought back into the middle and a new round begins as before. The team that scores the selected number of points first is the winner or the team with the most points after a certain number of rounds is the winner.

COMMENTS:
This game is very simple but very fun. Younger kids and some older kids will get a kick out of this. It's fun to watch and play. Try it!

Variant:

BATTLE VOLLEYBALL: This is the same game except one volleyball is used instead of several balloons. Kicking is not allowed and a larger field should also be used. If the volleyball hits the ground, a toss-up ensues and play continues. This takes a little more skill and teamwork than Balloon Volley, but it is equally fun!

BOMBARDMENT

NUMBER OF KIDS: 2 teams of 3 or more

AGES: 7 and up

TIME ALLOTTED: 40 minutes or more

PLAYING FIELD: a grassy or paved area that can be split into two even sides

---

EQUIPMENT: playground balls (usually 2 or 3 depending on the number of players) and however many pins (such as bowling pins, cones, tennis ball cans, or large plastic cups) are desired (usually 4 to 10 per team)

START-UP: Players should define boundaries that consist of a roughly square or rectangular area with a center line. Teams are then chosen. The balls are divided evenly between the two teams. An equal number of pins is set up along the back line of each side. Each team chooses and enters one side.

OBJECT: To knock down all of the opponents' pins.

PLAY: A designated player signals the start of the game. From that point on, the playground balls are thrown toward the opposing team. Players, however, are never allowed to cross the middle line. If a player is struck by a ball thrown by an opponent, the player that was hit is temporarily out of the game. That player must walk off to the side of the playing field. Players can run anywhere on their side within boundaries to dodge opponents' throws. A player is safe if the ball misses or strikes the ground before contact. A player may also catch a ball thrown by the other team. If a catch is made successfully, the thrower is out and the players who have been knocked out on the catcher's team reenter the game. If at any time a team is down to one player, that player cannot be eliminated by being hit but can still catch the ball. This rule allows for there to be at least one player on each team to guard pins at all times.

The most important factor in the game is the pins. While the above is taking place, the real goal (because it is impossible to win by eliminating everyone) is to knock down all the opponents' pins. Once a pin is knocked over, it cannot be set up again. The game continues until one team knocks down all the opposing teams' pins. The team that does so is the winner.

COMMENTS:

This game is a great variation on the classic dodgeball and is sometimes referred to as Pin Dodgeball. If kids are not afraid to get hit by a ball and are competitive, they will love this game. It is a load of fun, and helps work on reflexes and coordination. This was one of my personal favorites and will catch on throughout the neighborhood. The pins make a fantastic extra challenge to an already exciting game!

BROOM CHASER

NUMBER OF KIDS: 4 or more

AGES: any

TIME ALLOTTED: 20 minutes or more

PLAYING FIELD: any large, open, and safe area

EQUIPMENT: 1 broom

START-UP: Players should define boundaries and choose someone to be the broom chaser.

OBJECT: To be the last player tagged.

PLAY: The player who is chosen to be the broom chaser begins with the broom. The broom chaser counts out loud to a certain number and the game begins. The broom chaser then tries to tag people with the bristled end of the broom. If a player is tagged, then that player becomes a broom chaser as well. The players do not switch places but become a team. The original broom chaser still gets to hold the broom and does so at all times. The other broom chasers help by grabbing and holding other players while yelling, "Broom chaser!" The broom chaser can then come and tag the person that is being held. This continues until all players but one have become a broom chaser by being tagged with the broom. The last person who has not been tagged is the winner and is the broom chaser in the next round.

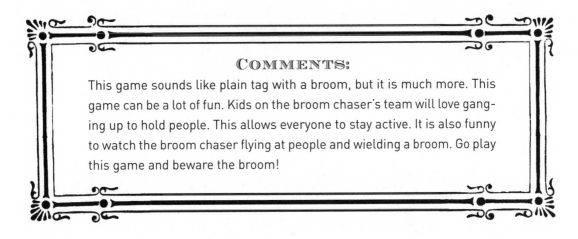

COMMENTS:

This game sounds like plain tag with a broom, but it is much more. This game can be a lot of fun. Kids on the broom chaser's team will love ganging up to hold people. This allows everyone to stay active. It is also funny to watch the broom chaser flying at people and wielding a broom. Go play this game and beware the broom!

CAPTURE THE COLORS

NUMBER OF KIDS: 2 teams of 4 or more

AGES: 8 and up

TIME ALLOTTED: 30 minutes or more

PLAYING FIELD: a large open area or field

EQUIPMENT: 1 makeshift flag for each player; each team must have matching flags

START-UP: Players should choose two teams and define boundaries. Each team selects a captain. Everyone places their flag in the back of their waistline, so that it hangs out and can be grabbed.

OBJECT: To get all of the other team's flags.

PLAY: Everyone scatters around the playing area and one player says, "One, two, three, go!" to signal the start of the game. The captains (and only the captains) try to capture the other team's flags. Everyone else simply tries to protect their own flag. If a player loses his or her flag, that player can help his or her captain by holding other players so the captain can more easily grab their flags. The first team whose captain grabs all the other team's flags is the winner.

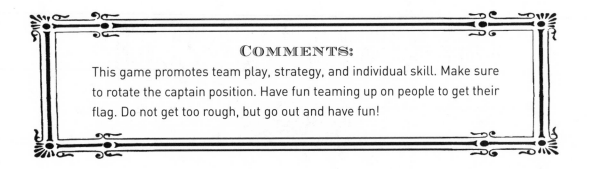

COMMENTS:

This game promotes team play, strategy, and individual skill. Make sure to rotate the captain position. Have fun teaming up on people to get their flag. Do not get too rough, but go out and have fun!

CAPTURE THE FLAG

NUMBER OF KIDS: 2 teams of at least 3

AGES: 7 or older

TIME ALLOTTED: 60 minutes or more

PLAYING FIELD: a large grassy or wooded area, such as connecting backyards or a park or a field with some trees

---

EQUIPMENT: 2 makeshift flags

START-UP: There are several variations on the rules to this game. Depending on the number of players, each can be tried. The fewer players there are, the simpler the game should be.

- **COMPLEX:** Players are split evenly into attackers, middlemen, and defenders.
- **MEDIUM:** Players are split evenly into attackers and defenders.
- **SIMPLE:** There are no set positions.

OBJECT: To gain points by stealing the other team's flag.

PLAY: Rules vary slightly depending on the level of complexity chosen, but the basic idea is consistent.

COMPLEX

In the complex version, the field is broken into three parts: two defense areas and a large area in the middle. Attackers and defenders split up into their own defense area. The middlemen from both teams begin in the neutral area.

Middle men are considered safe in the middle area and cannot be tagged. They may also never leave the middle area. The middlemen's job is to tag attackers from the other team when they enter the middle area.

Attackers may roam anywhere on the field. They are only safe in their own defense area and may be tagged anywhere else. Their job is to sneak past the middlemen and then past the other team's defense to try to steal the flag.

Defenders can only protect their own flag and cannot leave their own defense area. Defenders are always safe and may never be tagged. A defenders only job is to tag the opponents' attackers when they enter the defense area.

At any time an attacker can switch positions with a defender. Switches can only take place within one's defense area and by changing one attacker for one defender, so there are a set number of attackers and defenders at all times. To avoid confusion, middlemen cannot switch positions with anyone.

MEDIUM

In the medium version, there are no middlemen. Only one middle line is used to divide the field in half. Defenders must stay in their own defense area, but attackers can go anywhere. Attackers can be tagged only after crossing the middle line into the other team's defensive area. The number of defenders must remain constant on a side at all times, but a one-for-one switch with an attacker may be performed in the defense area.

SIMPLE

In the simple version, there are no attackers and no defenders, and only one middle line is used to divide the field in half. Any player is free to leave his or her side at any time, but that player is vulnerable to being tagged upon crossing the middle line.

RULES FOR ALL THREE

Before the game starts, a jail should be marked in one corner of each defense area and the flags planted anywhere in the defense area. Once the game begins, players can be tagged by opponents when they enter the nonsafe areas. Tagging is done literally when a defender or middleman tags an attacker. A tagged attacker must then throw up his or her hands to signal capture (faking this is not allowed!). The captured player then goes to the other team's jail. If more than one player is in jail, they form a line with the first player caught in the front. A player in jail can be released if another attacker manages to get to the jail and tag him or her. Only the first player in line in the jail can be freed, so only one player can be freed at a time. If a player is freed, that player must again throw up his or her hands and return to his or her own defensive area. Only then can the freed player once again attack.

Points are scored when an attacker manages to get a hold of the other team's flag and attempts to return the flag to the other side without being tagged. One point is scored for obtaining the flag and then being tagged. In the medium and simple versions, three points are scored for successfully returning to one's own defensive side with the flag before being tagged. In the complex version, one point is scored for obtaining the flag, two points for a return to the neutral territory, and three points for a successful return to the other defensive side. Handing off the flag to another attacker is allowed! However, after the player holding the flag is caught, or if the flag touches the ground, everyone returns to their own side (even players in jail), points are awarded, the flag is returned, and play starts again.

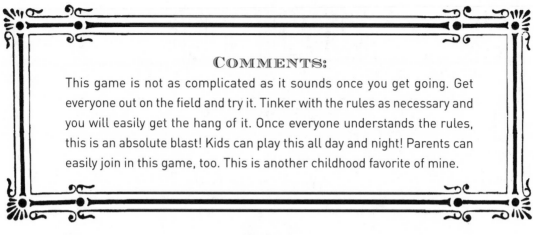

COMMENTS:

This game is not as complicated as it sounds once you get going. Get everyone out on the field and try it. Tinker with the rules as necessary and you will easily get the hang of it. Once everyone understands the rules, this is an absolute blast! Kids can play this all day and night! Parents can easily join in this game, too. This is another childhood favorite of mine.

Variant:

JAILBREAK (ALSO CALLED PRISONER'S BASE): This is basically the same game, but all prisoners can be freed at the same time. The trick here is that the attacker must put one or two feet in the jail and yell, "1, 2, 3, jailbreak!" before being caught. This frees all of the players in the jail. The other trick is that there are no free walks back to one's own side. Once a player dashes free from jail, that player is free to be captured again but is also free to capture the flag. This adds a little more intensity (as if it were needed!) and is a great time.

CHAIN TAG

NUMBER OF KIDS: at least 5

AGES: any

TIME ALLOTTED: 20 minutes or more

PLAYING FIELD: a small open area

EQUIPMENT: none

START-UP: Players should define relatively small boundaries and choose someone to be It.

OBJECT: To be the last player tagged.

PLAY: Everyone spreads out inside the boundaries. The It counts out loud to a certain number and the game begins. The It then attempts to tag anyone and everyone. If a player is tagged, that player must join hands with the It. Those players then attempt to tag more people together. If one of the Its tags someone, that player must join hands with the person who tagged him or her. If the chain breaks at anytime, no tags are allowed until the chain is rejoined. The game continues until only one player is left untagged. That player is the winner and becomes the initial It for the next round.

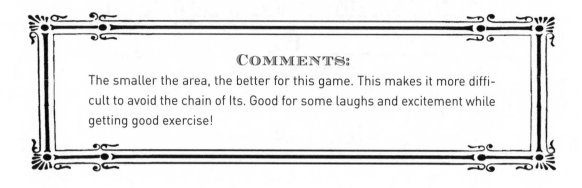

COMMENTS:

The smaller the area, the better for this game. This makes it more difficult to avoid the chain of Its. Good for some laughs and excitement while getting good exercise!

CHANGE DODGEBALL

NUMBER OF KIDS: 7 or more

AGES: 7 and up

TIME ALLOTTED: 30 minutes or more

PLAYING FIELD: a large open area or field

EQUIPMENT: 1 playground ball

START-UP: One player is chosen to be It and everyone else gathers in a circle around him or her.

OBJECT: To avoid being It.

PLAY: The It begins with the ball and throws it to another player (player 1). Player 1 throws the ball to another player (player 2). Player 2 throws the ball to another player (player 3). Player 3 throws the ball right back to the It. The trick to this game is the switch. As soon as player 2 throws the ball to player 3, players 1 and 2 must switch places in the circle. As soon as the It receives the ball from player 3, he or she tries to hit players 1 or 2 before they can get to their new location. If a player is hit during the switch, that player becomes It for the next round. If the It is unsuccessfully, he or she is It again. Passing to an adjacent person is never allowed! Play continues for as long as players want.

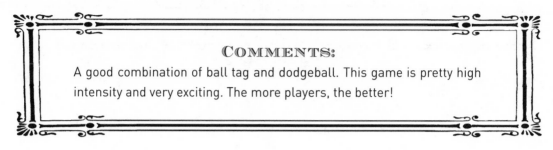

COMMENTS:

A good combination of ball tag and dodgeball. This game is pretty high intensity and very exciting. The more players, the better!

CIRCLE PASS

NUMBER OF KIDS: 4 or more

AGES: any

TIME ALLOTTED: 15 minutes or more

PLAYING FIELD: any open area

EQUIPMENT: none

START-UP: A circle is marked or drawn in the playing area and players spread out on the edge of the circle in a random order.

OBJECT: To be the last player remaining.

PLAY: One player says, "Ready, set, go!" and the game begins. All players begin walking fast or running around the circle (players should decide before the game if running is allowed). The object is to eliminate players by passing them. Passing may be completed on the inside or outside of a player, as long as the passer never enters the circle. If any player enters the circle at any time, that player is eliminated and must step inside the circle until the next round. If someone is passed, that player is eliminated and must step inside the circle until the next round. Players continue going around the circle, trying to pass one another, until only one is left. That player is the winner.

COMMENTS:

Games don't get easier than this to play. Try changing directions, walking backward, crawling, or letting smaller or slower players run to try to even the odds. This makes for great exercise, and it's easy and fun to play!

CIRCLE SURVIVOR

NUMBER OF KIDS: at least 3

AGES: any

TIME ALLOTTED: 15 minutes or more

PLAYING FIELD: a small, grassy area or small blacktop or concrete area

---

EQUIPMENT: 1 soccer ball or basketball for each child

START-UP: Players should define strict boundaries within a small grassy area. Each player should take one soccer ball and enter the defined area.

OBJECT: To be the last player with his or her ball inside the circle.

PLAY: Everyone counts to three and play begins. In this game, each player is responsible for his or her own ball. With no intentional physical contact, each player attempts to kick everyone else's ball out of the circle. If a player gets his or her ball kicked out of the circle, that player is eliminated from the game. When eliminated, the player must leave the circle. Play continues until everyone but one person has been eliminated. This player is the winner. Start another round!

An optional method of playing is to use a basketball that players must dribble and draw a circle on cement as the playing area. The rest of the rules are the same.

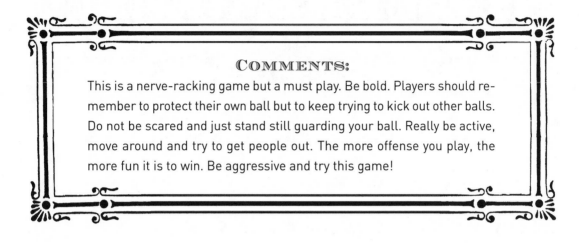

COMMENTS:

This is a nerve-racking game but a must play. Be bold. Players should remember to protect their own ball but to keep trying to kick out other balls. Do not be scared and just stand still guarding your ball. Really be active, move around and try to get people out. The more offense you play, the more fun it is to win. Be aggressive and try this game!

COMBINATION/CREATIVE TAG

NUMBER OF KIDS: 3 or more

AGES: any

TIME ALLOTTED: 20 minutes or more

PLAYING FIELD: any large area

EQUIPMENT: depends on the rules chosen

START-UP: Players should define boundaries and choose someone to be It. They then decide on which rules to follow. A combination can be done, such as combining the rules of Reverse Tag and Ball Tag (see game descriptions), or players can form unique rules on their own. This book describes several exciting versions of tag, but these are by no means every possibility. These can be used along with any other creative idea players have.

OBJECT: To avoid being It.

PLAY: Everyone spreads out inside the boundaries. The It counts out loud to a certain number and the game begins. As in regular tag, if a tag is made, that player becomes the new It. Designated rules must be followed at all times. The game continues until the players agree to stop.

COMMENTS:

Try this! Mix up different tag games to make them more original and challenging. Be creative! It can be fun to make the rules or just try a goofy combination of all the rules you know!

CRACK THE WHIP

NUMBER OF KIDS: at least 3

AGES: any

TIME ALLOTTED: 15 minutes or more

PLAYING FIELD: a large grassy field or yard free of hard or rough ground

EQUIPMENT: none

START-UP: Players choose an order for everyone. The first player is deemed the leader and the other players are followers. Everyone gets in order and joins hands with the people next to them (forming the whip). The leader and the player at the end can use two hands to hold on to the one person to whom he or she is connected.

OBJECT: The leader's goal is to shake everyone off the whip. Everyone else must hold on to the whip as long as possible.

PLAY: Once everyone is ready, the leader begins to run and everyone else must keep up without breaking the chain. The leader should start to run around in a crazy fashion, bobbing, weaving, and turning. After everyone is running at full speed and making sharp turns, the players toward the back will begin to fly off the whip because of the abrupt changes in movement. Slowly, everyone is tossed off the whip. Once most players have been thrown off the whip, mix up the order and play again. Try to play at least once from each position. The game really has no winner or end, but generally bragging rights go to the leader who shakes everyone off the fastest.

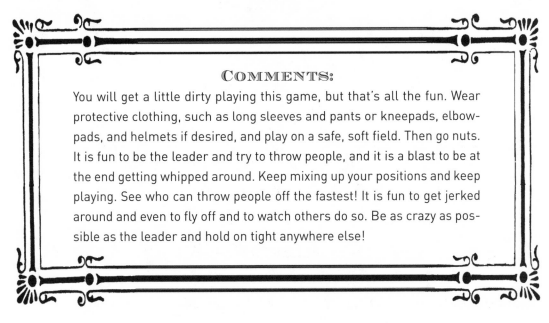

COMMENTS:

You will get a little dirty playing this game, but that's all the fun. Wear protective clothing, such as long sleeves and pants or kneepads, elbow-pads, and helmets if desired, and play on a safe, soft field. Then go nuts. It is fun to be the leader and try to throw people, and it is a blast to be at the end getting whipped around. Keep mixing up your positions and keep playing. See who can throw people off the fastest! It is fun to get jerked around and even to fly off and to watch others do so. Be as crazy as possible as the leader and hold on tight anywhere else!

DODGEBALL

NUMBER OF KIDS: 2 teams of at least 3

AGES: 7 and up

TIME ALLOTTED: 40 minutes or more

PLAYING FIELD: a large grassy or paved area that can be split into two even sides

---

EQUIPMENT: playground balls (usually 2 or 3 depending on the number of players)

START-UP: Players should define boundaries that should be square or rectangular area with a middle line. Teams are chosen and split onto opposing sides of the middle line. The balls are all set on the middle line and each team stands on the back line of its half of the playing field.

OBJECT: To have the last remaining player(s) in the game.

PLAY: Someone signals the start of the game. Players rush from the back line to get possession of the balls. The playground balls are then thrown at will toward the opposing team. Players are never to cross the middle line or go out of bounds. If a player is struck by a ball thrown by the other team, that player is temporarily out of the game and goes to sit on the side. Players can run anywhere within their half of the field to dodge the ball. A player is safe if a thrown ball misses or strikes the ground before contact. A player may also catch a ball thrown by the other team. If a catch is made successfully, the thrower becomes temporarily out, and everyone on the catcher's team that was temporarily out now rejoins the game. This continues until everyone on one side has been eliminated. The other team is the winner.

COMMENTS:

This was always one of my personal favorites and will catch on throughout the neighborhood. Although you will get hit by the ball, you'll be having so much fun that you'll hardly feel it!

Variant:

DOCTOR DODGEBALL: This game uses the same set of rules with two changes. The first change is that players sit down instead of leaving the field when they are hit. The second change is that one player from each team is designated a doctor before the game. The doctor can bring a player back into the game by touching him or her. The doctors can stand safely on the sidelines and may enter the playing field at will. Once the doctors enter the playing field, they can be eliminated like any other player. Once a doctor is eliminated, he or she is out of the game for good, and the game finishes in the same fashion.

Variant:

FREE-FOR-ALL DODGEBALL: In this game, every player tries to eliminate one another. There is no middle line, and all other rules apply. Catching the ball results only in the thrower being eliminated. The last player left wins.

Variant:

ALLEY DODGEBALL: Players separate into three teams, and split the playing field into three sections instead of halves. Two teams split into the outside areas and one team gets into the inside area. The outside teams try to hit the inside players with the balls. If a player is hit, that player is out and there is no reentry. Catches can be made and the catcher is safe. If a player in the middle grabs a ball at any time, that player should toss it back to an outside player. The last player still alive in the middle wins. Take turns with which team gets to be on the inside.

Variant:

SQUARE DODGEBALL: A square is formed for boundaries. One team must stay inside the square; the other must stay outside the square at all times. Players on the outside are on full-time offense and inside players are on full-time defense. If an inside player is hit, the outside team earns two points. If a ball is caught, the team does not score points. Balls that land or are caught inside must immediately be returned to the outside. Intentional failure to return a ball results in the outside team earning a point. One point is also awarded if an inside player crosses accidentally or purposefully to the outside of the square. After two minutes, the teams switch. Two or three rounds are played and the team with the highest score wins.

FLASHLIGHT TAG

NUMBER OF KIDS: at least 3

AGES: any

TIME ALLOTTED: at least 45 minutes

PLAYING FIELD: a large field with hiding places or several connecting yards in a neighborhood, or in a large park

EQUIPMENT: 1 flashlight for each It (can be 2 flashlights with many players)

START-UP: Players determine an area in which to play. Players then choose a base to tag or a line to cross to be safe. Last, players choose someone to be It.

OBJECT: To return safely to base without being revealed by the flashlight.

PLAY: Everyone begins at the base or safe line. The It waits there for at least one minute while the rest of the players run and hide within the determined area. After that time, the job of It is to find the hiders and to shine the flashlight on them. While the It is doing this, players attempt to sneak back to base or across the safe line without the It noticing them and shining the flashlight on them. If a hider successfully reaches the base, the hider announces it loudly and play continues. Play continues until the It catches someone who will replace them during the next round. If all hiders become safe, the last hider to come in is It for the next round.

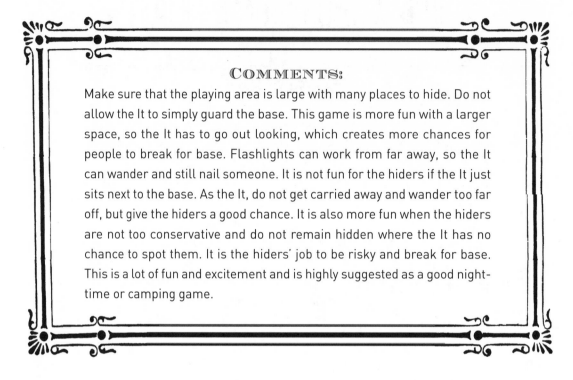

COMMENTS:

Make sure that the playing area is large with many places to hide. Do not allow the It to simply guard the base. This game is more fun with a larger space, so the It has to go out looking, which creates more chances for people to break for base. Flashlights can work from far away, so the It can wander and still nail someone. It is not fun for the hiders if the It just sits next to the base. As the It, do not get carried away and wander too far off, but give the hiders a good chance. It is also more fun when the hiders are not too conservative and do not remain hidden where the It has no chance to spot them. It is the hiders' job to be risky and break for base. This is a lot of fun and excitement and is highly suggested as a good night-time or camping game.

FRISBEE WAR

NUMBER OF KIDS: 3 or more

AGES: any

TIME ALLOTTED: 15 minutes or more

PLAYING FIELD: any decent-sized yard or field

EQUIPMENT: 1 Frisbee for each player

START-UP: Players define loose boundaries and each chooses a Frisbee.

OBJECT: To be the last person remaining that has an unflipped Frisbee.

PLAY: Play begins with all players throwing their Frisbees into the air. At first players may want to throw conservatively to ensure that their Frisbee does not land upside down. Eventually each player should start throwing his or her Frisbee to knock an opponent's Frisbee over on its back. If a player's Frisbee lands upside down, that player is eliminated. One exception is that no one can physically touch an opponent's Frisbee in any way. A player can only hit an opponent's Frisbee by throwing his or her own Frisbee. A player may catch his or her own Frisbee in midair or if it is rolling on its side, but if it comes to rest and is upside down, that player must sit out until next game. The winner is the last person remaining. Single games or a series can be played.

COMMENTS:

A good mix of defense and offense is key. It is good to throw conservatively, but it is also fun to fling your Frisbee toward an opponent's. So go be a little risky and have fun! This game is really a blast once you get good at tossing and controlling your Frisbee. It will probably seem hard at first, but it gets more and more entertaining with skill and experience.

HAND TAG

NUMBER OF KIDS: 3 or more

AGES: any

TIME ALLOTTED: 20 minutes or more

PLAYING FIELD: any decent-sized area

EQUIPMENT: none

START-UP: Players should define boundaries and choose someone to be It.

OBJECT: To avoid being It.

PLAY: Everyone spreads out in bounds. The It counts out loud to a certain number and the game begins. The It then tries to tag the other players. As in regular tag, if a tag is made, that person becomes the new It. The trick in this game is that the new It must keep one hand on the place where he or she was tagged (e.g., if tagged on the left shoulder, the new It must keep one hand on his or her left shoulder at all times until a tag is made). The next player tagged must do the same. The game continues for as long as the players want.

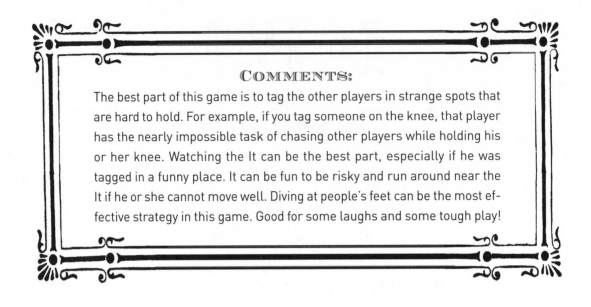

COMMENTS:

The best part of this game is to tag the other players in strange spots that are hard to hold. For example, if you tag someone on the knee, that player has the nearly impossible task of chasing other players while holding his or her knee. Watching the It can be the best part, especially if he was tagged in a funny place. It can be fun to be risky and run around near the It if he or she cannot move well. Diving at people's feet can be the most effective strategy in this game. Good for some laughs and some tough play!

INTERFERENCE TAG

NUMBER OF KIDS: 4 or more

AGES: any

TIME ALLOTTED: 20 minutes or more

PLAYING FIELD: any decent-sized open area

EQUIPMENT: none

START-UP: Players should define boundaries and then choose one player to be the runner and one to be the chaser.

OBJECT: To avoid being the chaser.

PLAY: Everyone spreads out inside the boundaries. The runner counts out loud to a certain number and the game begins. The chaser then tries to tag the runner. If successful, the runner becomes the chaser, and the former chaser instantly calls out another player's name. The person called becomes the new runner and play continues. The trick to this game is that, at any time, another player may run "interference" on the chase. This is accomplished by tagging the runner and yelling,

"Interference!" The interfering player instantly becomes the new runner until tagged or until someone else performs interference. The game ends when all players agree to stop.

COMMENTS:

This is a game that may seem atypical but is a load of fun. It can be played with just a few kids, but more players add more interfering and confusion, which adds to the fun. Go out and try it; it is a great game!

JACK, JACK, SHOW YOUR LIGHT

NUMBER OF KIDS: 4 or more

AGES: 8 and up

TIME ALLOTTED: 1 hour or more

PLAYING FIELD: a large semi-wooded area or park with places to hide

EQUIPMENT: 1 flashlight, 1 watch, and 1 whistle

START-UP: Play is best when it is dark or becoming dark outside. Players strictly define boundaries. One player is chosen to be Jack, who gets the flashlight and the whistle.

OBJECT: To catch Jack.

PLAY: Play begins by giving Jack a fifty-second head start into the woods. After this count, all other players scatter to look for Jack. Once the chase begins, Jack is required to show his or her flashlight every thirty seconds by turning it on, holding it straight out, and spinning in a circle. Players should yell, "Jack, Jack, show your light!" to inspire Jack to show the flashlight. When a player sees Jack's light, that player must yell, "Run, Jack, run!" to give Jack fair notice. If no one sees the light and yells, "Run, Jack, run!" Jack must stop, blow the whistle, and swing the flashlight continuously until someone spots the light and yells, "Run, Jack, run!" The game ends when someone catches Jack. If no one catches Jack after thirty minutes, Jack must stay still, blow the whistle, and leave the flashlight on until someone finds him or her. Whoever catches Jack first is Jack for the next round.

COMMENTS:

This is really an exciting game that keeps everyone moving and excited. It can be scary, exciting, and fun at the same time. Kids will get hooked on this game. The key is finding a good, safe area to play. This game will be a hit!

JUMP ROPE

NUMBER OF KIDS: 1 or more

AGES: any

TIME ALLOTTED: 20 minutes or more

PLAYING FIELD: an open paved area

EQUIPMENT: 1 or 2 jump ropes (slightly heavy ropes can be substituted)

START-UP: If there are three or more players, two rope spinners and one or more jumpers must be chosen.

OBJECT: To continually jump the rope(s).

PLAY: For only one person, the game is simple. The player simply takes one end of the rope in each hand and jumps rope. Once a player gets good, he or she can add challenges such as hopping on one foot, turning the rope underfoot twice on one jump, crossing arms, trying to bounce a small ball, or creating new tricks.

Three or more players can play double Dutch. Two ropes are needed. The two spinners each take one end of each rope in a different hand. They must spin one rope in one direction and the second rope in the opposing direction. The jumper(s) then jumps into the middle and must continuously jump both of the ropes. Some of the same tricks may be done in this game as well, plus players can create many more. Players can take turns by jumping in and out of the ropes or play can continue until a player is hit by one of the ropes. Spinners and jumpers should switch positions every few minutes so everyone can jump.

An option is that spinners can chant their favorite playground rhymes while spinning.

COMMENTS:
This is great exercise! It is also fun to be creative and try new tricks. The more you practice, the better you will get. Mastering new tricks is exciting, but even basic jumping can be a lot of fun.

KEEP-AWAY CHASE

NUMBER OF KIDS: 3 or more, or teams of 2 or more

AGES: any

TIME ALLOTTED: 15 minutes or more

PLAYING FIELD: a large area with obstacles, such as a playground or adjacent yards

EQUIPMENT: 1 object to hold, such as a small ball, toy, or handkerchief

START-UP: One object is chosen with which a player can easily run. One person or team is then picked to start with the object. Everyone else becomes chasers. Players then determine how the object holder(s) is caught—usually by tagging or putting both arms around him or her.

OBJECT: To possess the object for as long as possible.

PLAY: Everyone gives the object holder(s) a thirty-second head start and the game begins. The chasers then attempt to catch whoever has the object. If the object holder is caught, the object must be given to the chaser. Time must be allowed for the new object holder to escape, and then the game continues. If teams are used, the object may be passed from teammate to teammate until someone is caught and the other team becomes the object holder. The game continues until the players decide to stop.

COMMENTS:

This game can be spontaneously played almost anywhere. It's a good combination of tag and keep-away. It's a ton of exercise and a load of fun. Go play this one!

KING (OR QUEEN) OF THE HILL

NUMBER OF KIDS: at least 3

AGES: 10 and up

TIME ALLOTTED: 20 minutes or more

PLAYING FIELD: usually a grassy hill (but be creative!)

EQUIPMENT: none

START-UP: Finding a good, safe hill is the most challenging part. Anything else that a player can be atop and pulled down or away from safely will work. A king or queen is chosen and proceeds to the top of the hill. The rest of the players remain at the bottom.

OBJECT: To become the king or queen on top of the hill and stay there for as long as possible.

PLAY: The chosen king or queen signals the start of the game. The rest of the players then try to climb the hill and pull off the king or queen. When a king or queen is pulled off, everyone tries to take his or her place at the top. The struggle from then on is constant, with players always trying to get to the top and stay there. This game can last for a certain length of time and whoever is on top after that time is the winner. It may also simply be continuous until the players are too tired to keep playing.

COMMENTS:

This game can get a little rough, but if kids are responsible, it can be a lot of fun. Do not play if you do not enjoy physical activities and contact. This game allows children to gain some strength and stamina while enjoying good fun and competition. This is good for kids who like physical activity and do not mind getting a little dirty.

KINGS AND QUEENS

NUMBER OF KIDS: 4 or more

AGES: any

TIME ALLOTTED: 30 minutes or more

PLAYING FIELD: any large safe area

EQUIPMENT: 1 soft ball

START-UP: Players should define boundaries and choose someone to be It.

OBJECT: To be the last player to become an It.

PLAY: The It begins with the ball. Everyone spreads out in bounds. The It counts out loud to a certain number and the game begins. As in Ball Tag, the It attempts to hit other players with the ball. Players in this game must keep closed fists and are allowed to touch or block the ball only with their fists. If a player is hit on any part of their body except the fist, he or she also becomes an It. This player does not switch places with the It, but they become a team. The Its can all pick up the ball with their bare hands, run with it, and toss it to one another to hit other players and make more players Its. If given the chance, players who aren't Its can also hit or carry the ball with their fists, but the ball may never touch any other part of the body and the players must keep their hands in fists. This way they can try to keep the ball out of the hands of the Its. The game continues until all players but one have become Its. The last player remaining is the king or queen and is the first It in the next round.

COMMENTS:

This game is a blast and is a great for a lot of laughs. It is a good spin-off of Ball Tag. Being It and not It are both very exciting in this game. The element of passing between Its with the other players able to block and carry the ball is too much fun to pass up. This takes some strategy, teamwork, and practice. Get kids playing this game and they will love it!

MINI-TENNIS

NUMBER OF KIDS: 2, or 2 teams of 2

AGES: any

TIME ALLOTTED: 30 minutes or more

PLAYING FIELD: a tennis court, driveway, or open paved area

EQUIPMENT: 1 tennis ball and 1 racquet for each player and chalk if no tennis court is available

START-UP: Players get on opposing sides of the net, each standing in one opposing service box (or use both service boxes for team play). The service boxes are the boundaries for this game. Choose one player or team to serve first.

OBJECT: To score fifteen points first.

PLAY: Each point begins with a serve. Serves are simple bumps over the net into the opponent's box. After the ball lands, the returner then bumps it back to the server. A point is then played similar to tennis (the ball must land in bounds and can bounce a maximum of one time). The ball can never be hit hard; instead, placement and finesse must be used. Players may run anywhere on their side of the net and hit the ball while it is still in the air or after one bounce. A player wins the point when his or her opponent misses the ball and it bounces twice or when the opponent hits the ball into the net or out of bounds. Each point won is worth one point. Each player takes a turns serving five times. The winner is the first player to score fifteen points, but the player must win by at least two points.

If no tennis court is available, people can play with two boxes on a driveway or a court drawn on a paved area. Players can also have a gap between the boxes or have them touching. A makeshift net can be made if desired. Hands can also be used instead of racquets.

COMMENTS:

This game is addictive! It takes a lot of practice to get good, but try lobs and drop shots. Use placement and strategy. The better you become, the more fun it is. Tons of fun and more exercise than you would possibly imagine!

NUTMEG

NUMBER OF KIDS: at least 3

AGES: any

TIME ALLOTTED: 20 minutes or more

PLAYING FIELD: a small grassy area

EQUIPMENT: 1 soccer ball for each child

START-UP: Players should set strict boundaries within a small grassy area. Each player takes one soccer ball and enters the defined area.

OBJECT: To be the last player remaining.

PLAY: One person counts to three and play begins. Players then attempt to kick any ball through another player's legs. A player does not have to keep the ball with which he or she began. Players may use or steal others' balls as well as their own. Hands cannot be used. No pushing, holding, or kicking is allowed, but a player can do anything else to kick a ball through another's legs. If a player has a ball kicked through his or her legs, that player is eliminated and must step out of bounds. If a ball goes out of bounds, the people who have been eliminated put it back into play, or a short time out is called to retrieve it. Play continues until everyone but one person has been eliminated. That player is the winner. Start another round!

COMMENTS:

This is high intensity and a must play. Try to be bold. Players should protect their own legs but be sure to attack others' as well. Do not be timid and just stand with your legs together. Really be active, move around, and try to get people out. The more offense you play, the more fun you will have. Give this game a shot!

OBSTACLE COURSE

NUMBER OF KIDS: 1 or more

AGES: any

TIME ALLOTTED: at least 30 minutes

PLAYING FIELD: anywhere where children have, or can build, obstacles to safely move over, through, and around, such as a playground

EQUIPMENT: anything safe

START-UP: Setting up the course is a fun part of this game. Players should invent their own obstacle course. They can use preexisting objects like trees, or they can place or build their own. Find a good area and be creative.

OBJECT: To finish the obstacle course, or to do it the fastest.

PLAY: Once the obstacle course is created, each player should take turns attempting to complete it. If desired, players can time one another to see who finishes the fastest. One player can conquer a course alone just for the challenge too.

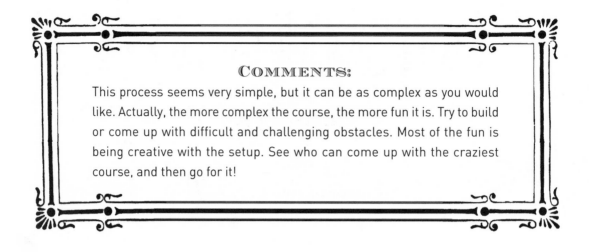

COMMENTS:

This process seems very simple, but it can be as complex as you would like. Actually, the more complex the course, the more fun it is. Try to build or come up with difficult and challenging obstacles. Most of the fun is being creative with the setup. See who can come up with the craziest course, and then go for it!

RACES

NUMBER OF KIDS: 2 or more

AGES: any

TIME ALLOTTED: 15 minutes or more

PLAYING FIELD: anywhere safe

EQUIPMENT: usually none, but depends on the race decided

START-UP: Players should decide on the type of race desired and determine a start and finish line.

OBJECT: To finish the race first or the fastest.

PLAY: There is a plethora of racing possibilities, because almost anything can be a race. Some common races include making teams of two and racing in a wheel-barrow position, or leapfrog racing, racing bikes, and racing around the house. These can all be a blast and provide entertainment for many kids, but any type of race may be performed. Players can race one at a time and try to make the best time, or they can race against each other at the same time to see who can finish first.

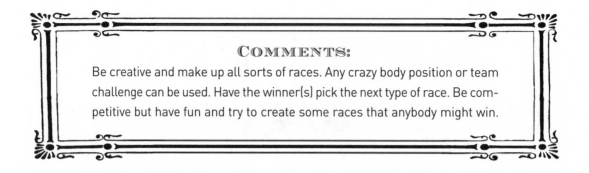

COMMENTS:

Be creative and make up all sorts of races. Any crazy body position or team challenge can be used. Have the winner(s) pick the next type of race. Be competitive but have fun and try to create some races that anybody might win.

REVERSE TAG

NUMBER OF KIDS: 3 or more

AGES: any

TIME ALLOTTED: 20 minutes or more

PLAYING FIELD: any decent-sized area

EQUIPMENT: none

START-UP: Players should define boundaries and choose someone to be It.

OBJECT: To avoid being It.

PLAY: Everyone spreads out in bounds. The It counts out loud to a certain number and the game begins. As in regular tag, if a tag is made, the tagged player becomes the new It. The trick in this game is that everyone must run backward at all times, even the It. The game continues until the players agree that they want to stop.

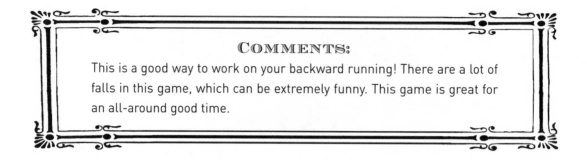

COMMENTS:

This is a good way to work on your backward running! There are a lot of falls in this game, which can be extremely funny. This game is great for an all-around good time.

SCORPION TAG

NUMBER OF KIDS: at least 3

AGES: any

TIME ALLOTTED: 20 minutes or more

PLAYING FIELD: a small grassy area

EQUIPMENT: none

START-UP: Players should define strict boundaries (usually small to even the odds). Someone is chosen to be the scorpion.

OBJECT: To avoid being the scorpion.

PLAY: The scorpion gets into a position like a scorpion (walking belly-up on hands and feet). The other players spread out in bounds. The scorpion then counts out loud to a certain number and the game begins. The scorpion then tries to tag other players, but must stay in the correct position at all times. A tag is made by touching another player with a raised leg (like a scorpion stinging). If tagged, that player is the new scorpion and the game continues. The game ends when the players agree to stop.

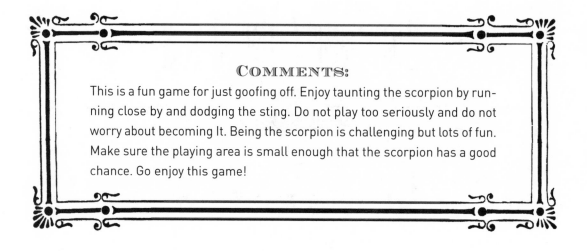

COMMENTS:

This is a fun game for just goofing off. Enjoy taunting the scorpion by running close by and dodging the sting. Do not play too seriously and do not worry about becoming It. Being the scorpion is challenging but lots of fun. Make sure the playing area is small enough that the scorpion has a good chance. Go enjoy this game!

SKRAG

NUMBER OF KIDS: 3 or more

AGES: 10 or older

TIME ALLOTTED: at least 20 minutes

PLAYING FIELD: a large grassy field or yard free of hard or rough ground

EQUIPMENT: a soft football

START-UP: Players should select a ball and define boundaries. One player starts with the ball.

OBJECT: To stay on his or her feet and avoid everyone else (for the person with the ball), and to tackle the player with the ball (for everyone else).

PLAY: Play begins with everyone getting into a circle. Whoever has the ball throws it up into the air. Whichever player feels bold enough grabs the ball and runs. Every other player then tries to tackle whoever grabbed the ball, for as long as it takes to do so. Once tackled, the tackled player throws the football back up into the air. Another player then grabs it, and play continues as before. The ball is not allowed to be passed or fumbled. If fumbled, the player who dropped it should immediately retrieve the ball or be tackled anyway. The game ends when everyone is too tired to continue.

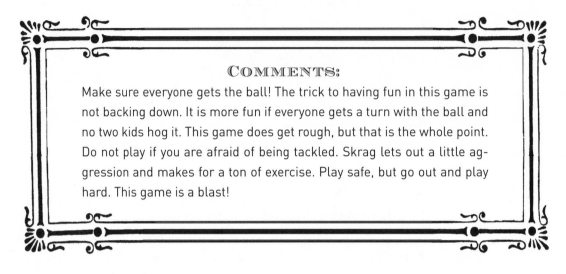

COMMENTS:

Make sure everyone gets the ball! The trick to having fun in this game is not backing down. It is more fun if everyone gets a turn with the ball and no two kids hog it. This game does get rough, but that is the whole point. Do not play if you are afraid of being tackled. Skrag lets out a little aggression and makes for a ton of exercise. Play safe, but go out and play hard. This game is a blast!

SMALL HOCKEY

NUMBER OF KIDS: 2 teams of at least 2

AGES: 8 and up

TIME ALLOTTED: 45 minutes or more

PLAYING FIELD: the end of a cul-de-sac is optimal, but any blacktop or concrete area will do if it is safe and can have goals placed on each side

---

EQUIPMENT: 1 hockey stick for each child, at least 1 rubber street hockey ball, 2 goals (makeshift or bought), and any appropriate safety equipment

START-UP: A field of play is chosen by the players, goals are set at each end, and teams are decided. The ball is set in the middle.

OBJECT: To outscore the other team.

PLAY: One player from each team faces off to begin the game. This is done by having one player from each team slap their sticks together three times above the ball, then try to take possession of it. This game's rules are similar to regular hockey without the checking and rough play. Passing and dribbling the ball with the stick are legal (using hands is not, except for the goalie). One player usually plays goalie, and the rest split up into offenders and defenders. Everyone then attempts to score. If a goal is made, the scoring team gets one point and another face-off ensues. If the ball goes out of bounds, the team that did not knock it out gains possession. Teams can play timed periods or until a certain score is reached.

COMMENTS:

This game is fantastic! I spent many an after-school afternoon playing this with friends. It can satisfy every kid for an entire afternoon. It is great exercise, teaches team lessons, and develops a lot of good sports skills. Once kids get into it, they will want to play for a long time. It takes time to get good, but getting better and better makes the games more and more exciting. Kids will come back thrilled after this game.

Variant:

ROLLER HOCKEY: The rules are the same except everyone but the goalies wear in-line skates.

Variant:

BROOM HOCKEY: The rules are also the same except brooms are used instead of sticks and a larger ball must be used (such as a playground ball). Also, play is usually on grass for this variant.

SMALL SOCCER

NUMBER OF KIDS: 2 teams of at least 2

AGES: any

TIME ALLOTTED: at least 30 or 40 minutes

PLAYING FIELD: a good-sized yard or field

EQUIPMENT: 1 soccer ball and makeshift goals

START-UP: A field of play is chosen by the players and small goals are set up. Goals can be anything from two posts on a fence to two cones set on the ground. Teams are picked. A coin flip or "rock, paper, scissors" is used to decide who starts with the ball. At the beginning of the game and after every goal, each team begins on their own goal line.

OBJECT: To outscore the other team.

PLAY: Rules of regular soccer apply but are not as strict (for example, off-sides is usually not a penalty in small soccer). Teams should have defenders and offenders, but these players may go anywhere on the field. There is usually no goalie because of the small goals and field. This is a simple game of dribbling, passing, and scoring. One team starts with the ball at its goal line and brings it up the field. Each team then tries to control the ball and score through the other team's goal. When a team is scored on, that team begins with possession of the ball, both teams return to their goal line, and play resumes. Teams can play timed periods or can play until a certain score is reached.

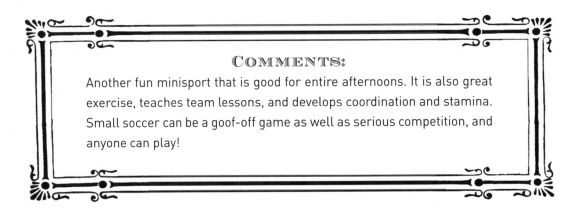

COMMENTS:

Another fun minisport that is good for entire afternoons. It is also great exercise, teaches team lessons, and develops coordination and stamina. Small soccer can be a goof-off game as well as serious competition, and anyone can play!

TAIL-GRABBERS

NUMBER OF KIDS: at least 7

AGES: any

TIME ALLOTTED: 25 minutes or more

PLAYING FIELD: a good-sized open area

EQUIPMENT: 1 makeshift tail for every 2 or 3 children

START-UP: Players should define boundaries and choose one or more tail-grabbers (depending on the number of players). Everyone else splits into even groups of two or three. Each group gets into a line, holding the hips of the person in front of them. The player in the back of each line wears the tail for his or her team. This is done by tucking the tail into a pants waistline so that it is hanging out.

OBJECT: To be the last team with their tail.

PLAY: Everyone gets inside the boundaries. The tail-grabber says, "Go!" and the game begins. The tail-grabber then attempts to pull the tail off each team. If a team loses its tail, the players are out of the game. A team can lose its tail if a tail-grabber pulls it off, or if a player breaks the chain by releasing the hips of the player in front of them. The last team with its tail is the winner. One of the winners gets to be the tail-grabber for the next round.

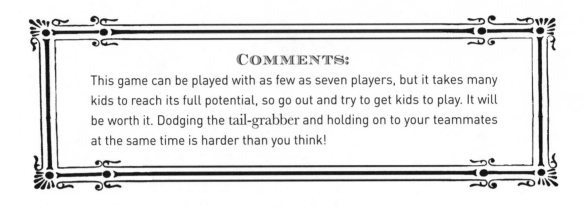

COMMENTS:

This game can be played with as few as seven players, but it takes many kids to reach its full potential, so go out and try to get kids to play. It will be worth it. Dodging the tail-grabber and holding on to your teammates at the same time is harder than you think!

THIRTY-TWO TIPS

NUMBER OF KIDS: at least 2

AGES: 7 and up

TIME ALLOTTED: 30 minutes or more

PLAYING FIELD: any area with a basketball hoop

EQUIPMENT: 1 basketball

START-UP: Players choose the area to play and decide which player gets the ball first. Choosing the first player can be done with a shootout at the free-throw line.

OBJECT: To be the first to score thirty-two points.

PLAY: The player with the ball checks it by passing the ball to another player and he or she passes it back, and the game begins. Each player then tries to score thirty-two points. Using basic basketball rules, if any player makes a basket, that player gets the ball back and the game continues. Fouls and two- and three-pointers apply, as in regular basketball. If a player misses a basket, two things can happen. Any other player can grab the ball and score. If a player is able to tip the ball in, that player gets the basket, and the player who shot the original shot has his or her score erased to zero. Tipping the ball requires a player to catch the rebound and shoot it in successfully while being in midair. This process continues until one player reaches thirty-two points and wins the game.

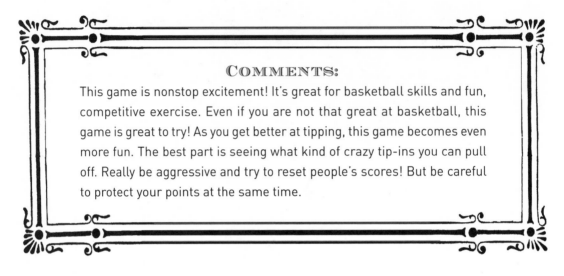

COMMENTS:

This game is nonstop excitement! It's great for basketball skills and fun, competitive exercise. Even if you are not that great at basketball, this game is great to try! As you get better at tipping, this game becomes even more fun. The best part is seeing what kind of crazy tip-ins you can pull off. Really be aggressive and try to reset people's scores! But be careful to protect your points at the same time.

THREE-COURT SOCCER

NUMBER OF KIDS: 2 teams of 4 or more

AGES: any

TIME ALLOTTED: 45 minutes or more

PLAYING FIELD: a good-sized, open grassy field

EQUIPMENT: 1 or 2 soccer balls (players' choice)

START-UP: Players should define boundaries of a large rectangular area broken up into five sections. There should be one large section in the middle and a slightly smaller end zone on each end. There also needs to be a small strip (of about five or ten feet) of neutral area in between the central area and each end zone. Choose teams. One team gets into the middle and the other team splits evenly between the end zones. The team in the end zones is the offense.

OBJECT: To score the most points.

PLAY: One player on the offense starts with the ball on the outside edge of one end zone. That player passes the ball to a teammate in that box and the point begins.

If two balls are used, one ball should start at each end. Once the ball is passed in bounds, the offense must then attempt to pass the ball across the middle area to a teammate in the other end zone. The ball must be passed along the ground. The defense is allowed to stop the balls by any means necessary without leaving their middle area. The offense also cannot leave its designated area. If the offense successfully passes the ball through the middle to another player in the other end zone who stops the ball in the end zone, it scores one point. If a pass goes through the middle area and through the other end zone and out of bounds, or if it is stopped by the defense, the ball is dead. The ball is then returned to the offense, again set at the back of the end zone, and passed in bounds. When a point is scored, another point immediately starts by setting the ball on the end zone line and passing it in bounds. After five minutes, the teams switch. Each team gets two rounds as offense. Whoever has the most points at the end wins.

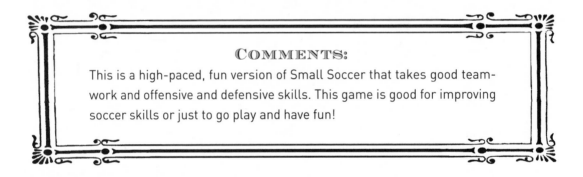

COMMENTS:

This is a high-paced, fun version of Small Soccer that takes good teamwork and offensive and defensive skills. This game is good for improving soccer skills or just to go play and have fun!

TOUCH FOOTBALL

NUMBER OF KIDS: 2 teams of 2 or more

AGES: any

TIME ALLOTTED: 45 minutes or more

PLAYING FIELD: a good-sized, open grassy field

EQUIPMENT: 1 football

START-UP: Players should define boundaries of a large rectangular area with an end zone on each end. Choose teams. One team is chosen to kick off and each team goes to opposite sides of the field.

OBJECT: To score the most points.

PLAY: One team kicks off to the other team by kicking, punting, or throwing the ball. The other team then tries to run the ball toward the other end zone. This team is the offense. The offensive player with the ball is down when he or she is touched with two hands by any defensive player. Following basic football rules, teams then attempt to score touchdowns. On offense, usually only one player is quarterback and the rest are receivers. The quarterback can either pass, hand off the football for another player to run, or he or she can run once every four downs; however, players are allowed to cross the line of scrimmage after counting to 5 and can try to tag the quarterback. Once a defender crosses the line, the quarterback can also run the ball. On defense, players should attempt to stop the offense by covering the receivers and quarterback. Defensive players cannot hold players and must touch any player with the ball with two hands to end the play. Incomplete passes also end a play. The offense can get a first down by going approximately ten yards or by completing two passes; players decide. On fourth down, the offense can punt the ball to the other team or may try one last time for a first down. If an offense team member is able reach the end zone successfully with the ball at any time, his or her team receives one point. This team must then kick off to the other team. The first team to reach a given number of points, usually five, is the winner. Teams can also play for a certain length of time, such as twenty-minute halves, and whoever has the most points is the winner.

COMMENTS:

This game is a true classic that every child should know. This can provide entertainment for hours. It is great exercise that can inspire interest in an organized sport. Get out and there and try it!

Variant:

ONE-CHANCE FOOTBALL: In this game, the same rules apply but the offense gets limited downs to score and a much smaller field must be used. One variant can be that offenses get no first downs, so they only have four chances to score. Another variant can be that each team only gets one down to score. This must be done on a field that is only about ten yards long. Teams take turns trying to go the whole ten yards.

ULTIMATE

NUMBER OF KIDS: 2 teams of 3 or more

AGES: 8 and up

TIME ALLOTTED: 45 minutes or more

PLAYING FIELD: a large grassy field

EQUIPMENT: 1 Frisbee

START-UP: Players should define a large field with designated sidelines, goal lines, and end zones. Teams are then decided.

OBJECT: To score the most points by making touchdowns.

PLAY: Teams begin on opposite sides of the field. One team begins by "throwing off" to the other team. This is done when one teams throws the Frisbee down the field toward the other team. The receiving team catches or picks up the Frisbee and the game begins. The team with the Frisbee is now on offense. They must advance the Frisbee up the field by throwing it to one another. Once a player has possession of the Frisbee, that player is not allowed to move with it. He or she can only throw the Frisbee to another player. To score, teams must advance the Frisbee all the way across the goal line and into the end zone. The defensive team is always trying to take possession of the Frisbee. Intentional contact is not allowed, but anything else goes. The defenders may guard the other players and try to intercept the Frisbee in the air. If the defenders gain possession of it, they become the offense and attempt to advance in the opposite direction. If the Frisbee should hit the ground at any time, the defending team takes possession. If any team member catches the Frisbee in the end zone successfully, he or she scores a touchdown and gets one point for the team. As in football, the teams return to their sides and the team that scored throws off the Frisbee and the game continues. The game can be played by quarters or halves, and whoever scores the most touchdowns wins. The game may also end when a certain score is reached.

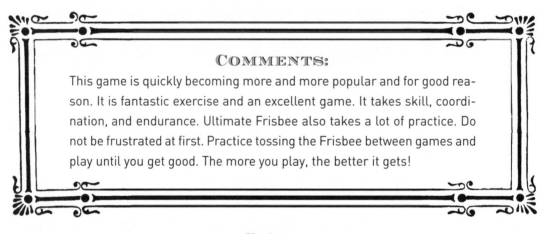

COMMENTS:

This game is quickly becoming more and more popular and for good reason. It is fantastic exercise and an excellent game. It takes skill, coordination, and endurance. Ultimate Frisbee also takes a lot of practice. Do not be frustrated at first. Practice tossing the Frisbee between games and play until you get good. The more you play, the better it gets!

Variant:

BOUNDARY BALL: Rules are basically the same except a chosen ball is passed in lieu of the Frisbee. Also, a score is made by rolling the ball across the goal line (the ball must be on the ground!). For this, smaller goals must be set up with cones in the middle of the goal lines. If the roll is unsuccessful, the defending team automatically takes possession.

WATER FIGHTS

NUMBER OF KIDS: at least 2

AGES: any

TIME ALLOTTED: 30 minutes or more

PLAYING FIELD: a yard, front and back, or a grassy outdoor area with water or hose access

EQUIPMENT: water guns, buckets, water balloons, cups, hoses (be creative!)

START-UP: Each player should gather all the supplies he or she desires before the game and prepare them as necessary. Enough supplies should be gathered to enable the game to last for a while (but breaks can be taken to stock up and to refill, of course). Boundaries can be set if desired. Teams are chosen or play can be a free-for-all.

OBJECT: To get the other people as wet as possible and to just have fun.

PLAY: In this game, there are really no rules that apply, except there is no rough-housing or physical play allowed. Each kid uses the supplies any way he or she sees fit to soak the other people or team(s). Reloading with more water is always acceptable. Play ends whenever the players decide to stop.

COMMENTS:

Great for a hot day or just to take out extra energy in a positive way. The more stuff you can use, the better. Be creative; get some buckets and anything else that could be good to launch water and go out and have fun!

YOU'RE UNDER ARREST!

NUMBER OF KIDS: 3 or more

AGES: 8 and up

TIME ALLOTTED: at least 1 hour

PLAYING FIELD: a large, safe neighborhood or biking area

EQUIPMENT: 1 bike for each child and any necessary safety equipment (such as helmets)

START-UP: Players should define large boundaries, roughly the size of three neighborhood blocks. A base is also chosen as the jail. One person is chosen to be the criminal (or two if there are many players). Everyone else is police.

OBJECT: To catch the criminals and bring them back to jail.

PLAY: Everyone begins at the jail. Once a criminal is chosen, he or she is allowed a two- to three-minute head start on his or her bike into the playing area. The police then split up and ride out to find the criminal. To capture a criminal, the police must ride up next to him or her and say, "You're under arrest!" Tagging is not permitted because a player could knock someone off the bike and cause serious injury! If arrested, the criminal must ride to base with the police officer. The game ends when each criminal is caught.

It is important for the police to check back to base every few minutes to see if the criminals have been caught. This prevents players from riding around looking for criminals when there are none left. It also ensures the next round will begin as soon as possible. Whichever police officer caught the criminal is then the next criminal.

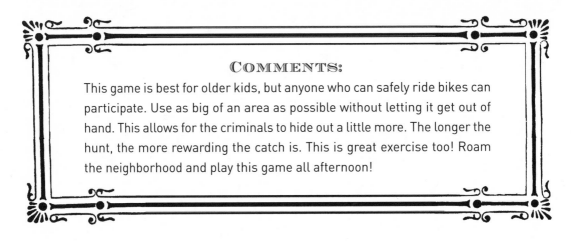

COMMENTS:

This game is best for older kids, but anyone who can safely ride bikes can participate. Use as big of an area as possible without letting it get out of hand. This allows for the criminals to hide out a little more. The longer the hunt, the more rewarding the catch is. This is great exercise too! Roam the neighborhood and play this game all afternoon!

INDEX

ABOUT THE AUTHOR

Scott Strother received his B.A. from the University of Notre Dame in psychology and preprofessional studies. He currently works for a non-profit company researching child development and education. He is also completing a Ph.D. researching child development through the University of Louisville.